AWARD MONOLOGUES FOR MEN

The effectiveness of a performance is always influenced by the quality of the writing. We wanted to provide a treasure-house for actors of wonderful speeches with unique practical tips on how to perform them. We trust this collection of 54 monologues from plays nominated for:

- the Pulitzer Prize
- the Tony Award
- the Drama Desk Award
- the Evening Standard Theatre Award
- the Laurence Olivier Award

will help all of you who are looking for up-to-date speeches for auditions, acting class, or who just want to enjoy extracts from some of the new plays that have arrived in the last 25 years.

– Patrick Tucker and Christine Ozanne

Patrick Tucker is Director of the Original Shakespeare Company and author of *The Actor's Survival Handbook* (with Christine Ozanne, 2005), *Secrets of Screen Acting* (2nd edition, 2003) and *Secrets of Acting Shakespeare – the Original Approach* (2002).

Christine Ozanne is an actor, co-founder of the Original Shakespeare Company and co-author of *The Actor's Survival Handbook*.

AWARD MONOLOGUES FOR MEN

Edited by Patrick Tucker and Christine Ozanne

Routledge
Taylor & Francis Group

LONDON AND NEW YORK

First published 2007 by Routledge
2 Park Square, Milton Park, Abingdon, Oxon OX14 4RN

Simultaneously published in the USA and Canada
by Routledge
270 Madison Ave, New York, NY 10016

Routledge is an imprint of the Taylor & Francis Group, an informa business

Typeset in Parisine by
Keystroke, 28 High Street, Tettenhall, Wolverhampton

Printed and bound in Great Britain by TJ International Ltd, Padstow, Cornwall

British Library Cataloguing in Publication Data
A catalogue record for this book is available from the British Library

Library of Congress Cataloging in Publication Data
Award monologues for men / chosen and edited by Patrick Tucker
and Christine Ozanne.
    p. cm.
Includes bibliographical references and indexes.
1. Monologues. 2. Acting. 3. American drama—20th century.
4. English drama—20th century. 5. Men—Drama.
I. Tucker, Patrick, 1941– II. Ozanne, Christine.
PN2080.A96 2007
812'.045089286—dc22   2007012395

ISBN10: 0–415–42837–8 (hbk)
ISBN10: 0–415–42838–6 (pbk)
ISBN13: 978–0–415–42837–8 (hbk)
ISBN13: 978–0–415–42838–5 (pbk)

Award Monologues for Men

Fifty-four speeches from plays that have won, or been nominated for, major Awards in New York and London from 1980 onwards; or from a performance by an actor similarly honoured.

Chosen and edited by Patrick Tucker and Christine Ozanne

This book of various and varied speeches is dedicated to our various and varied siblings:

Martin, Nicholas, Elisabeth, Andrew and Gordon.

CONTENTS

INTRODUCTION

This book contains over 50 speeches.

These monologues are to help you:

1   to find a really good audition piece;
2   to find a suitable piece for classes which extend and improve your acting;
3   to find pieces that give you range and opportunity;
4   to see a selection of pieces from some well written plays.

SOURCES

Plays first presented since 1980, with the latest having its first performance in 2005.

WHICH

Those plays that have won or been nominated for major Theatre Awards in New York and London, or contain a speech performed by a similarly awarded actor. Two-thirds of the plays chosen are by American authors.

WHY AND HOW

We wanted all the speeches to come from well-written plays, and have read 328 of the 336 plays so nominated, plus most of the additional 199 plays that contain nominated performances. Because they are all plays connected with Awards, the writing is of a high standard – and we all know that the better the writing, the better your performance will be.

TEXT

We have reproduced the text exactly as it appears in the published script. Sometimes other characters have lines, but in all cases it is possible to perform the piece without someone else saying them.

DETAILS

The speeches are collected into four age-bands, and each speech has full details of when and where it was first performed and by whom, plus background details as to the character and situation.

NOTES

We have included specific notes and helpful hints at the bottom of each speech, along with definitions of any unusual words or references. There is a separate list of numbered notes for general use, and some Quick Advice on Auditioning.

LISTS

We have made a record of all the plays listed in the main New York and London Theatre Awards from 1980 to 2006, so you can see where the plays and playwrights come from, and when it was they received their accolades. We have also included an Index to all the plays used, plus all the individual actors who originally performed the speeches.

ACKNOWLEDGEMENTS

The idea and inspiration for these two related books (there is a companion volume *Award Monologues for Women*) comes from our long-time publisher and friend William Germano, who has been a constant supporter of our work.

Our editors at Routledge, Talia Rodgers and Minh Ha Duong, have been very helpful and supportive to the mammoth task of getting all the plays and permissions together.

Our research into the Award plays was mostly done at what we found to be the best source of play scripts in London, the library of the Royal Academy of Dramatic Art, whose staff were extremely helpful.

All the pieces in this volume are copyrighted, and the acknowledgements are given with each speech, where there are the details of who holds the copyright, and for which territory where appropriate. The holders of those rights wish to make it clear that you will need to seek permission for any public performance of these pieces, as well as any reproduction or photocopying of the work. The Owner's copyright in all these pieces shall be reserved.

For the work of Neil Simon, professionals and amateurs are hereby warned that 'Laughter on the 23rd Floor' and 'Lost in Yonkers' are fully protected under the Berne Convention and the Universal Copyright Convention and are subject to royalty. All rights, including without limitation professional, amateur, motion picture, television, radio, recitation, lecturing, public reading and foreign translation rights, computer media rights and the right of reproduction, and electronic storage or retrieval, in whole or in part and in any form, are strictly reserved and none of these rights can be exercised or used without written permission from the copyright owner. Inquiries for stock and amateur performances should be addressed to Samuel French Ltd., 52 Fitzroy Street, London W1P 6JR. All other inquiries should be addressed to Gary N. DaSilva, 111 N. Sepulveda Blvd., Suite 250, Manhattan Beach, CA 90266–6850, mail@garydasilva.com

HOW TO USE THIS BOOK

FIVE DIFFERENT WAYS OF FINDING A SPEECH:

1 Go to the **Contents** (page vii) to find the age bracket that suits you.
2 Go to the **Index of Playwrights** (page 151) to look up a specific writer.
3 Go to the **Index of Plays** (page 152) to look up a particular play.
4 Go to the **Index of Actors** (page 153) to look up what speech was originally performed by an actor similar to the type you are looking for.
5 Read through the speeches in your chosen age bracket to find the one that suits your purposes.

The text is as the author intended, with standardised stage instructions in italics inside square brackets. There has been no editing – all the other characters' lines are included, and the spelling (American or English) is as in the original text.

The speeches are arranged according to the age of the character: 20s, 30s, 40s, and over 50s, and then by alphabetical order of playwright. At the beginning of each section, all the speeches in that age range are listed.

DETAILS OF THE SPEECHES

At the top of each speech we name the author, and when it was first performed in a major city. The awards which the play or the performance gathered are listed, as is the character's name, and who first performed it. The age range for the character is listed according to the author (or failing further information, the age of the original actor who created the role), but these can often be just guidelines, and you should not feel restricted to looking only at those roles in your actual age range.

The type required for the part is stated, as well as a brief note as to the situation from where this speech comes. This is not gone into in great detail, as your performance will not be a re-creation of what you might do were you to be performing the role, but as a launch pad and platform for you to display all your acting abilities, and thrill the auditioners, and yourself, with the sheer joy of acting. A speech by itself cannot have the same effect as the same speech in the context of the play, and so it cannot be performed just as a slice of that play.

We have made a few comments at the bottom of each speech, including an explanation of any unusual words, and refer to the numbered **Notes on speeches** where applicable.

Although certain parts may be written for specific backgrounds of nationality, race or class, do not let this stop you from using one that will show YOU off to your best advantage, simply because you do not fit the exact requirements as asked for by the author.

QUICK ADVICE ON AUDITIONING

We, as director (Patrick) and actor (Christine), have participated as performer and/or adjudicator in hundreds of classes, workshops, competitions, and auditions. Our advice and notes are drawn from these experiences.

1   The people judging you will be your 'audience' and need to be entertained as such.
2   If you need to announce the name of the piece you are doing, make it short: character, play title, author. There really shouldn't be any need to 'set the scene'. Exceptions should be only where appropriate, but whatever you do keep it brief and natural (not 'recited').
3   Start at once. Do not spend time getting into character; do not stand there with your eyes closed, breathing deeply and so on. Just get on with it. In other words, make an impact right from the start.
4   Use the simplest costume possible required for the character.
5   Use only those props that are absolutely necessary. Do not mix real props and mimed props in the same piece. Either one or the other.
6   Never apologize in advance for anything. Health problems, especially with the voice, will be obvious enough. *Never* give any hint that you don't know the piece very well, whatever the excuse might be. Again it will be obvious enough if you don't. If you have to take a prompt do it with aplomb, and don't come out of character. *Never re-run a line, just plough on regardless.* Chances are they won't notice your mistake if you do it with skill and confidence.
7   If you have to start again, either at their request or yours, try to do it differently to show what a flexible actor you are.
8   Be sensitive to the auditioners' remarks, don't argue a point, treat their comments as good advice.

9   Have an amusing anecdote ready if it refers to the audition piece, but only use it if you feel absolutely sure it will get a favourable reaction. Otherwise leave, quickly and cheerfully.

10 Before you begin, imagine that you have just done the audition and you are now going to do it even better!

NOTES ON SPEECHES

We realise that many of the notes we will be giving you will be repeated for different speeches, so instead of duplicating all the information onto each page, we give here all our main notes, numbered as **Note 1**, **Note 2**, etc. and then for each speech we will give some specific notes, followed by: **See Note 1**, **See Note 2** and so on, as appropriate.

NOTE 1   OTHER CHARACTER'S LINES

All the text is included. You can leave a gap where the other person is speaking, as it gives you a chance to do some good 'listening' acting. You can either act the information in the other lines, or add a few words so that the audience will know what it was that they were saying – such as putting them in the form of a question at the start of your next speech. A good alternative is to act the second character yourself, with a strong indication that this is what you are doing, such as using a change of voice. This can be a very effective short-cut to clarifying the other lines.

NOTE 2   LENGTH AND STYLE OF SPEECH

We have printed the speech up to a natural ending point, but it may be a little too long for your particular needs. Be unashamed in cutting a monologue down to suit those talents and abilities you wish to present or to work on – that is more important than presenting a coherent story.

NOTE 3   CONFUSING OR RUDE WORDS

Be happy to change any reference in the speech to one your audience will understand, such as place names or a specific cultural reference. If the language in the piece is inappropriate for your purposes (such as the use of profanities or swear words), then again be happy to change it.

NOTE 4 JOURNEY

Make sure your character goes on a journey, and that you end up in a different place to where you began. To stay the same leads an audience to wonder why they bothered to watch you, as you have not changed from first to last. If your character appears not to change in the speech, then make sure that the audience have gone on a learning journey as they watch your acting; someone must change, so if it is not you, then it must be the audience. Try not to be consistent – it is the enemy of good acting. If you hit one note and stay on it, the audience can easily guess the conclusion – and if they get there before you do it, it is a bored audience.

NOTE 5 THEORY OF OPPOSITES, AND SURPRISES

If you are to do something, do the opposite first. If you are about to be happy, then find a truthful way of being sad just before; if sad, then find a reason for your face to be smiling just before the 'sad' thought occurs. This will make the moment clearer and more fun for the audience to understand and enjoy. Also, try to find an unexpected way to deliver a line or certain word to surprise the audience. Let all interruptions catch you by 'surprise'. This is a good technique, especially at auditions.

NOTE 6 TALKING TO THE AUDIENCE

If you are alone on stage, then a few muttered words can be spoken as if to yourself – but a long speech never can: it is a soliloquy.

There are two schools of thought about how to deal with a soliloquy – you can either speak to a 'generalised' audience, never exactly catching anyone's eye, or you can speak to the audience directly. Some auditioners are uncomfortable if you include them in this, so if you plan to do so, check beforehand that this is going to be acceptable.

NOTE 7   ACCENTS AND VOICE

If the speech requires an accent which is not your natural one, be sure that you have a good reason for choosing it. Make sure you can sustain the accent effortlessly throughout, as any suspicion that you are not totally at ease with it will reflect badly in your performance, and good acting energy can be wasted on maintaining an accent. This also applies to 'character' voices that are not natural to you.

NOTE 8   STAGING

Always place the person you are speaking to downstage, so that when you talk to them the people watching you can see the changing thoughts on your face. If necessary, place chairs downstage of you to indicate where these other people will be.

NOTE 9   USE OF PROPERTIES (PROPS) AND COSTUMES

Either use real props, or mime them all. You do not have to have the exact prop, just something that will stand in for it. Doing a speech that leaves a broken prop onstage is not a good idea. An exception to mixing real and imaginary props is for food and drink, which are best mimed, for handling them when auditioning can be impractical. It is usually not a good idea to have a full costume, but an element of the correct one (a coat, a scarf, a hat) can be used to good effect.

20s

1	**Jon Robin Baitz**	TEN UNKNOWNS	Judd
2	**Bill C. Davis**	MASS APPEAL	Mark
3	**Bruce Graham**	COYOTE ON A FENCE	Bobby
4	**Richard Greenberg**	THE AUTHOR'S VOICE	Gene
5	**Ron Hutchinson**	RAT IN THE SKULL	Roche
6	**Howard Korder**	BOYS' LIFE	Phil
7	**Tony Kushner**	ANGELS IN AMERICA: MILLENNIUM APPROACHES	Louis
8	**John Leguizamo**	FREAK	Johnny
9	**Kenneth Lonergan**	THIS IS OUR YOUTH	Dennis
10	**Martin McDonagh**	THE PILLOWMAN	Katurian
11	**Terrence McNally**	LOVE! VALOUR! COMPASSION!	Ramon
12	**Michael Murphy**	SIN (A CARDINAL DEPOSED)	Patrick
13	**Peter Shaffer**	AMADEUS	Mozart
14	**Nicky Silver**	PTERODACTYLS	Todd
15	**Neil Simon**	LAUGHTER ON THE 23RD FLOOR	Ira
16	**Anna Deavere Smith**	TWILIGHT: LOS ANGELES, 1992	Michael
17	**Tom Stoppard**	ARCADIA	Valentine
18	**Hugh Whitemore**	IT'S RALPH	Dave
19	**August Wilson**	JITNEY	Shealy
20	**Lanford Wilson**	ANGELS FALL	Zappy
21	**Mary Zimmerman**	METAMORPHOSES	Phaeton

1

TEN UNKNOWNS

Jon Robin Baitz

FIRST PERFORMANCES	New York 2001
AWARDS	Justin Kirk nominated for the *Drama Desk Award for Outstanding Featured Actor in a Play.*
CHARACTER	Judd
PLAYED BY	Justin Kirk
CHARACTER'S AGE	late 20s
TYPE	A rising young painter, and addict.
TIME AND PLACE	1992; an artist's decrepit studio in a village in Mexico.
SITUATION	Judd, a young painter, has been sent by the art dealer Trevor to help Malcolm Raphelson prepare new paintings for a major retrospective of his work. He is confronting his mentor about being cruelly treated, and suggests that his own work be used for the retrospective.

Judd: Shut up. I just want one thing: To know why? *[Beat.]* Why on earth did you do this to me? Look at me. This is what you've done. *[Beat. RAPHELSON can not speak. Totally articulate and clear-headed. He goes on, shaking his head, still baffled.]* Why? Malcolm. The public nature of it. As soon as there were other people to witness this – you turned – The satisfaction. You made fun of me with Trevor, to my face, and worse, with her too. Any opportunity for indignity, humiliation: 'Cabbages for hands,' erasure, rewriting history to your own specs . . . why? All the things you hated. The prospect of New York. Of what you would do to me – at a retrospective, in a gallery. Yow. I can imagine it – your constant digs and with so many people there – I don't understand it. I don't. Can you please try and explain it. *[Beat. JUDD is in tears. He shakes his head.]* I'm sorry if I . . . *[Beat.]* Did something – if I seemed – disrespectful or . . . *[Beat. There is silence. JUDD tries to pull himself together. He shakes his head.]* I keep trying to figure out why you would possibly want to do this and I can't even – *[Beat.]* I wasn't around for all the years you watched yourself become invisible and more and more marginal . . . It must have been . . . *[He stops. He nods. Suddenly clear to him.]* I know what it is. *[Beat. Simply amazed.]* Take my work – sell it . . . and sell it as your own – and you get your revenge on everyone – me – because I can actually paint – and these people whom you loathe, who did this to you. It's so malignant. It's brilliant and twisted. You get everything you want. That's what this is. Revenge on all of us. *[Pause.]* You're a comic book villain, do you know that, Malcolm? And in case you hadn't noticed – up there – back in New York, they've declared that painting is dead. You have no idea how tiny the stakes are. *[JUDD is suddenly absolutely certain and direct and compelled.]* But you know who I am? I am a mute with great feeling, huge battles going on inside, storms, plagues . . . but no way to express any of it. These useless skills. To execute a . . . but otherwise impotent, nothing else. *[Beat.]* I loved you Malcolm, I would sit here and understand exactly what you wanted, what you were trying to do. Just a nod or a shake or twitch from you was enough. Fantastic. Magic. Collaboration, the sum bigger than the parts, I was never better, you were never braver – and however it worked – when we were together, something great – But then, alone, when I went off, I went through pad after pad, now I was fucked . . . but all of it a blur, worthless. Dead. Nothing to say. Torn paper.

NOTES FOR THIS SPEECH:

'retrospective': art exhibit or exhibition showing an entire phase of an artist's lifework.

Feel free to change words if necessary: See Note 3.

You start off on a high, and end up emotionally drained: See Note 4.

You have a wonderful moment of great realization, that you are the better painter, and it must show: See Note 5.

2

MASS APPEAL

Bill C. Davis

FIRST PERFORMANCES	New York 1980; London 2006
AWARDS	Nominated for the *Drama Desk Award for Outstanding New Play*.
CHARACTER	Mark
PLAYED BY	Eric Roberts [US]; Brendan Patrick [UK]
CHARACTER'S AGE	early 20s
CHARACTER'S TYPE	He is a young trainee Catholic priest.
TIME AND PLACE	Today; America, Sunday Mass in Father Farley's church.
SITUATION	Father Farley's comfortable life style (and comfortable wealthy congregation) are disturbed when an intense seminarian comes into their parish with his idealism, to deliver his first sermon.

Mark: Thank you, Father Farley. *[MARK faces the congregation.]* It's funny – I never stopped to think that on my way to becoming a priest: I'd have to live with the name, Deacon Dolson. It sounds pretty silly, don't you think? 'Deacon Dolson.' *[A single cough – He freezes.]* Can I ask all of us a question? Why did we come to mass today? What brought us to church this morning? As a teenager I had a friend who answered this question by saying, 'I go to mass because my parents go.' But one day I heard his father talking to my father: 'Betty and I go to mass for the kids.' *[Several coughs are heard.]* I know when I was young, I liked going to church because right after mass my father would take us to the bakery. And all four of us – my two sisters and my brother and myself – would pick out what we'd like. I'd almost always get jelly doughnuts, and I'd never wait to get home before having one . . . *[Two loud coughs from the congregation.]* But jelly doughnuts aren't a very good reason for going to mass are they? *[Many coughs.]* What are your reasons . . . *[Several coughs. MARK erupts.]* I wonder if the coughing lot of you know, or *try* to know why you pull yourselves out of bed every Sunday morning and come here!? *[Silence.]* Do you need to come to mass? Do you need the church? Ideally, the purpose of the church is to become obsolete. But until it is, we need the habit of coming together and collectively recognizing that there is another world. There is a world that coexists and gives order to this world. Individually we come to mass with our own personal chaos and together we look to be ordered. We must come with our hearts open for that. *[Cell phone chirps.]* But you come with your designer shirts and your cell phones and your blue hair . . . Those things are your shackles – they are accessories you have *made* essential. *You* are essential.

NOTES FOR THIS SPEECH:

The building of the coughs you hear must be done by building your reaction to them, getting increasingly angry. The first half of the speech is what you have carefully prepared, the last part what you really believe: **See Note 4**.

Being really full of happy memories at eating jelly doughnuts will give a nice contrast to the next bit: **See Note 5**.

Apart from the first four words, this speech is given to the audience: **See Note 6**.

3

COYOTE ON A FENCE

Bruce Graham

FIRST PERFORMANCES	Cincinnati 1998; New York 2000; London 2004
AWARDS	Paul Sparks nominated for the *Drama Desk Award for Outstanding Actor in a Play*.
CHARACTER	Bobby
PLAYED BY	Jordan Matter; Paul Sparks [US]; Alex Ferns [UK]
CHARACTER'S AGE	late 20s
CHARACTER'S TYPE	He is skinny, pale and with a pronounced limp; illiterate, and a member of the Aryan nation (a neo-fascist group).
TIME AND PLACE	Now; on death row in a southern prison in America.
SITUATION	He is talking to his neighbour, an educated prisoner called John.

Bobby: No, this is gonna' make ya feel better, honest. See that fellah – he was . . . evil. A predator. Wasn't he? Tried to steal from ya – took advantage of your . . . your weakness. That's a predator. And there's nothin' wrong with killin' a predator.

John: Thank you, Bobby, thank you. Of course you will tell this to the pardon's board for me, won't you?

Bobby: That's in the Bible, John.

John: Lotta' stupid crap in the Bible –

Bobby: Ol' Hew said it too. He wouldn't steer me wrong predators must be destroyed. They have coyotes where you grew up?

John: No.

Bobby: Nasty animals. Can ruin a rancher, pickin' on the stock. Wipe out a whole chicken house in one night. Ranchers, man, they hate 'em. Hate coyotes more than anything. *[Quiet for a moment, thinking back.]* I know, I seen it. Just got outta' the hospital 'cause'a my hip –

John: What happened to it?

Bobby: Got smashed up –

John: How?

Bobby: Just did –

John: How?

Bobby: Just did! So my mother – the whore – I tell 'er wanta' go to Uncle Hew's but she – heck – she couldn't got me there if she wanted to and this man's she with, he . . . so I walked – *[Laughs.]* Well, limped. Six miles outta' town – man-oh-man it hurt – didn't have no aspirin or nothin'. Just wanted to get to my uncle's and I'm gettin' close I can see the lights out there and . . . man-oh-man, almost peed myself – 'cause there's this . . . monster! And it's floatin' in the air there, and I can see its eyes and – *[Laughs.]* Well, lemme tell ya, John: If there was a limpin' race in the Olympics, I'd of won it that night. I burst in on poor Hew shakin' and cryin' and heck – he didn't even know I was comin' but he hugged me there and put me in the truck and drove on out there. Coyote – that's all it was – stuck up on the barbed wire there. I figure it got caught in the fence till ol' Hew showed me the bullet hole. He'd shot it and stuck it up there. Beat on it too, while it was wounded. So we went back, he fed me, put me ta bed – but he sees I'm still upset 'bout it. Ya know how kids don't wanta' see any animal get hurt. So he sat there onna' bed and told me 'bout coyotes bein' evil and predators and how it's okay ta kill 'em and there's nothin' to he ashamed of. That's why he stuck it up onna' fence there. Let the world know – death to predators. *[Simply.]* Then he told me all about the Jews. How Hitler knew they were predators and about the cabal and everything. How they was usin' the niggers and mud people to turn us all into animals so they can enslave us. *[Laughs sadly, remembering.]* Uncle Hew, he had a beautiful voice. Could'a been on the radio. So, couple days later, he takes me out to Mr. George's – 'member him, the bike guy? Terrence George, George Terrence? Well he had this big garage like out in the middle of the woods. Musta' been a hundred people there: old, young, babies feedin' on their moms and . . . and Mr. George calls me up to the front there and asks if I'll swear my allegiance. And I say 'sure' and so we do it and . . . John, I look back and ol' Hew, he's smilin'. He's so proud'a me. And I walk down the aisle there . . .

And, John, they all reached out. Shakin' my hand, pattin' me on the back . . . huggin' me . . . *[Savoring it.]* Ol' Hew beamin' back there and all this . . . love. They was reachin' out for me, John. Reachin' out . . . You make peace with yourself, John. And write anything ya want 'bout me. Don't matter. I am a lucky man, John. A lucky man . . . *[He smiles dreamily.]*

NOTES FOR THIS SPEECH:

The initial conversations can be easily acted by you: **See Note 1**.

The whole is quite long, and you may want to trim it, by leaving out the beginning interchanges, or by leaving out the section at the end on you going to Mr George's: **See Note 2**.

Some of the words are offensive, so feel free to change any if they would be inappropriate for your needs: **See Note 3**.

The speech starts with pain, and ends with happiness; make sure you make as big a change as you can: **See Note 4**.

This needs an accent from the American countryside: **See Note 7**.

4

THE AUTHOR'S VOICE

Richard Greenberg

FIRST PERFORMANCES	New York 1987, 1999
AWARDS	Philip Seymour Hoffman nominated for the *Drama Desk Award for Outstanding Featured Actor in a Play*.
CHARACTER	Gene
PLAYED BY	David Hyde Pierce; Philip Seymour Hoffman
CHARACTER'S AGE	late 20s
TYPE	Misshapen recluse, who smells, with literary brilliance.
TIME AND PLACE	Now; Todd's apartment in New York.
SITUATION	Gene writes the books that Todd takes credit for, in return for being looked after. Now, against Todd's orders, Gene has taken a trip outside to gather more background for his writings.

Gene: It came to me: Why not? *[Beat.]* You were gone and I wasn't physically restrained. The outside world might be a painful place but every place is a painful one, so why not? *[Beat.]* I put on your greatcoat and your glasses and your fedora and looked almost hardly abnormal at all. I was careful, Todd, don't look at me like that, I was so careful, no neighbor saw, not the super, no one, I walked in shadows *exclusively. [He smiles hopefully.]* I know you've taken me on at great financial and personal sacrifice to yourself, I know I've altered your life completely. I know with me on your hands no sane life is possible, I'm grateful, I truly am, I'm not an ingrate, *don't look at me like that! [Beat. He picks up the books.]* I got these at a used-book store, a place, I swear to you, as musty as myself. I fit right in.

[Beat.] Todd, I had to do this for both of us. I was forgetting things; words lost their attachments. Without this little trip, this one, one-time-only little trip, you would have had a book full of nonsense, a mere *crunch* of syllables. *[Beat.]* It's not a place I want to go to any more, the world. I promise. *[Beat.] This isn't fair! [Beat.]* Look: burn this coat, buy another on our royalties! Another hat, too, and new glasses, I know I'm an infection, I won't be insulted! Please, please talk! I'm sure I must have been laughed at on the street, you don't have to worry . . . *[Beat.]* Please . . .

NOTES FOR THIS SPEECH:

'ingrate': ungrateful person.

This character gives you a great opportunity to create a very different physical type.

The gear changes are sudden, and give you a chance to really create different moods: See Note 5.

You can use real books, or mime them: **See Note 9**.

5

RAT IN THE SKULL

Ron Hutchinson

FIRST PERFORMANCES	London 1984; New York 1985
AWARDS	Nominated for the *Laurence Olivier Award for Best Play of the Year*.
CHARACTER	Roche
PLAYED BY	Rufus Sewell [UK]; Colum Convey [US]
CHARACTER'S AGE	late 20s
CHARACTER'S TYPE	He is a committed Irish terrorist.
TIME AND PLACE	1980s; British police interrogation cell in London.
SITUATION	Roche has been pulled in for questioning following a bomb blast in the UK, and he is battling with the techniques used to try to force a confession out of him. He is alone in the cell, after being beaten up by the police.

Roche: *[He smokes a cigarette hooked under his palm, jail-bird and corner-boy style. His testimony is measured, sly, almost humorous.]* Dear Mum, this is me in London Town. I've seen all the sights, the Tower, the Zoo, McDonald's and the bottom sides of coppers' boots from the wrong way up.

They showed me the doings. I was sat on my hunkers, minding my own business, wondering whether to pick my nose or go for a slash and a sledge-hammer comes through the door, without so much as by your leave. Followed in short order by half a dozen of the larger size of bobby, waving guns and shouting hallo.

One of them shakes me by the balls and throws me across the room before I've a chance to say I didn't catch the name and I'm not that inclined even so, and then it's down the stairs, the Human Brick and into the Paddy Wagon, through the black arse end of which many a good man before yours truly has found himself, and never a reason given him neither.

Then in comes the massed bands of the Metropolitan Police shouting hallo again, sit on my head by way of keeping me company to Paddington Green, and could you ask for a nicer nick, five stars and crossed truncheons. They grow these London coppers big, believe me. They like them big and ugly.

But fair play – never a hand on me after the arrest. The violence of the tongue, yes, and excited waving of the shooters but nothing more than that except the odd gag about why don't we save the taxpayer the cost of keeping the sod the rest of his natural and heave him arse over tit out of the back of the van?

But they meant no harm by it. What's new about taking the rise out of a poor bewildered Paddy? A bit of sport. Great crack. Not a hand on me. Not even the hand of the one who lost a brother to a brick in Derry in seventy-two.

Mind you, he turns a worrying shade of green when I say as soon as I'm back home I'll look up the hand of the man that threw the brick and shake it hard. But that was just my bit of sport. My crack. He knew I meant no harm by it – though it did take six of them to keep him off your loving son, Michael Patrick de Valera Demon Bomber Roche.

NOTES FOR THIS SPEECH:

'Paddy Wagon': police van;

'Paddington Green': armoured police station in London to which suspected terrorists are taken;

'De Valera': Leader of republicans during Irish War of Independence in the 1920s. Later President of Ireland, 1959 – 73.

If any of the words confuse, be willing to change them: See Note 3.

Your natural humour can give a lot of fun to the nice language you have to describe the nasty things they were doing to you: See Note 5.

It should be in an Irish accent, although American accents fit the rhythm well: See Note 7.

For the purposes of an audition, using both a cigarette and a postcard may be too much; you can mime them: See Note 9.

6

BOYS' LIFE

Howard Korder

FIRST PERFORMANCES	New York 1988; London 2005
AWARDS	Nominated for the *Drama Desk Award for Outstanding New Play*.
CHARACTER	Phil
PLAYED BY	Steven Goldstein [US]; James Witt [UK]
CHARACTER'S AGE	20s
CHARACTER'S TYPE	He is vulnerable and innocent, and socially inept.
TIME AND PLACE	Now; a bench in a New York park.
SITUATION	Friends since college, the three men, Phil, Jack and Don, are meeting up and swapping tales of their adventures, amorous and otherwise.

Phil: I would have destroyed myself for this woman. Gladly. I would have eaten garbage. I would have sliced my *wrists* open. Under the right circumstances, I mean, if she said, 'Hey, Phil, why don't you just cut your wrists open,' well, come on, but if *seriously* . . . We clicked, we connected on so many things, right off the bat, we talked about God for *three hours* once, I don't know what good it did, but that *intensity* . . . and the first time we went to bed, I didn't even touch her. I didn't *want* to, understand what I'm saying? And you know, I played it very casually, because, all right, I've had some rough experiences, I'm the first to admit, but after a couple of weeks I could feel we were right there, so I laid it down, everything I wanted to tell her, and . . . and she says to me . . . she says . . . 'Nobody should ever need another person that badly.' Do you *believe* that? 'Nobody should ever . . .'! What is that? Is that something you saw on TV? I dump my *heart* on the table, you give me Joyce Dr Fucking Brothers? 'Need, need,' I'm saying I *love* you, is that wrong? Is that not allowed anymore? *[Pause.]* And so what if I did need her! Is that so bad? All right, crucify me, I needed her? So *what*! I don't want to be by myself, I'm by myself I feel like I'm going out of my mind, I do. I sit there, I'm thinking forget it, I'm not gonna make it through the next *ten seconds*, I just can't *stand* it. But I do, somehow, I get through the ten seconds, but then I have to do it all over again, 'cause they just keep coming, all these . . . seconds, floating by, while I'm waiting for something to happen, I don't know what, a car wreck, a nuclear war or something, that sounds awful but at least there'd be this *instant* when I'd know I was alive. Just once. 'Cause I look in the mirror, and I can't believe I'm really there. I can't believe that's me. It's like my body, right, is the size of, what, the Statue of Liberty, and I'm inside it, I'm down in one of the legs, this gigantic hairy leg, I'm scraping around inside my own foot like some tiny fetus. And I don't know who I am, or where I'm going. And I wish I'd never been born. *[Pause.]* Not only that, my hair is falling out, and that really *sucks*.

NOTES FOR THIS SPEECH:

Adjust the language if it is too strong for your needs: See Note 3.

Let us believe you have a really important conclusion to it all, until you talk about your hair: the final sentence being really 'down to earth' making an amusing contrast to the rest of the speech: See Note 5.

You could position two chairs for the bench, which could be at an angle to the audience, and move around to talk to your friends from behind at some stage: See Note 8.

7

ANGELS IN AMERICA: MILLENNIUM APPROACHES

Tony Kushner

FIRST PERFORMANCES	San Francisco 1991; London 1992; New York 1993
AWARDS	Won *The Pulitzer Prize for Drama*; and the *Tony Award for Best Play*; and the *Drama Desk Award for Outstanding New Play*; nominated for the *Laurence Olivier Award for Best New Play*.
	Marcus D'Amico nominated for the *Laurence Olivier Award for Actor of the Year*.
	Joe Mantello **won** the *Drama Desk Award for Outstanding Featured Actor in a Play*; nominated for the *Tony Award for Best Actor in a Featured Role in a Play*.
CHARACTER	Louis
PLAYED BY	Michael Ornstein [US]; Marcus D'Amico [UK]; Joe Mantello [US]
CHARACTER'S AGE	20s
TYPE	A word processor for a law firm, and closet homosexual.
TIME AND PLACE	Early 1990s; Coffee shop at an outpatients' clinic, New York.
SITUATION	Louis is with his partner Prior, who is dying from AIDS and now on a drip. Belize is a black ex-dragqueen, and now caretaker for Prior.

Louis: *Power* is the object, not being tolerated. Fuck assimilation. But I mean in spite of all this the thing about America, I think, is that ultimately we're different from every other nation on earth, in that, with people here of every race, we can't . . . ultimately what defines us isn't race, but politics. Not like any European country where there's an insurmountable fact of a kind of racial, or ethnic, monopoly, or monolith, like all Dutchmen, I mean Dutch people, are well, Dutch, and the Jews of Europe were never Europeans, just a small problem. Facing the monolith. But here there are so many small problems, it's really just a collection of small problems, the monolith is missing. Oh, I mean, of course I suppose there's the monolith of White America. White Straight Male America.

Belize: Which is not unimpressive, even among monoliths.

Louis: Well, no, but when the race thing gets taken care of, and I don't mean to minimalise how major it is, I mean I know it is, this is a really, really incredibly racist country but it's like, well, the British. I mean, all these blue-eyed pink people. And it's just weird, you know, I mean I'm not all that Jewish-looking, or . . . well, maybe I am but, you know, in New York, everyone is . . . well, not everyone, but so many are but so but in England, in London I walk into bars and I feel like Sid the Yid, you know I mean like Woody Allen in *Annie Hall*, with the payes and the gabardine coat, like never, never anywhere so much – I mean, not actively despised, not like they're Germans, who I think are still terribly anti-semitic, and racist too, I mean black-racist, they pretend otherwise but, anyway, in London, there's just . . . and at one point I met this black gay guy from Jamaica who talked with a lilt but he said his family'd been living in London since before the Civil War – the American one – and how the English never let him forget for a minute that he wasn't blue-eyed and pink and I said yeah, me too, these people are anti-semites and he said yeah but the British Jews have the clothing business all sewed up and blacks there can't get a foothold. And it was an incredibly awkward moment of just . . . I mean here we were, in this bar that was gay but it was a *pub* you know, the beams and the plaster and those horrible little, like, two-day-old fish and egg sandwiches – and just so British, so *old*, and I felt, well, there's no way out of this because both of us are, right now, too much immersed in this history, hope is dissolved in the sheer age of this place, where race is what counts and there's no real hope of change – it's the racial destiny of the Brits that matters to them, not their political destiny, whereas in America . . .

Belize: Here in America race doesn't count.

Louis: No, no, that's not . . . I mean you *can't* be hearing that . . .

Belize: I . . .

Louis: It's – look, race, yes, but ultimately race here is a political question, right? Racists just try to use race here as a tool in a political struggle. It's not really about race. Like the spiritualists try to use that stuff, are you enlightened, are you centred, channelled, whatever, this reaching out for a spiritual past in a country where no indigenous spirits exist – only the Indians, I mean Native American spirits and we killed them off so now, there are no gods here, no ghosts and spirits in America, there are no angels in America, no spiritual past, no racial past, there's only the political, and the decoys and the ploys to manoeuvre around the inescapable battle of politics, the shifting downwards and outwards of political power to the people . . .

NOTES FOR THIS SPEECH:

'payes': Jewish ritual side curls (sometimes spelled 'payess').

This piece is about power, and so the sexuality of the character is irrelevant; perform it any way you want.

You can incorporate Belize's lines into yours: See Note 1.

Feel free to trim the piece to suit you, and to change words if necessary: See Notes 2 and 3.

The piece ends where Belize interrupts you, but for your purposes you should make it a grand finale to a good build full of varieties: See Notes 4 and 5.

8

FREAK

John Leguizamo

FIRST PERFORMANCES	New York 1998
AWARDS	Nominated for the *Tony Award for Best Play*.
	John Leguizamo nominated for the *Tony Award for Best Actor*.
CHARACTER	Johnny
PLAYED BY	John Leguizamo
CHARACTER'S AGE	late 20s
CHARACTER'S TYPE	He is the son of a Latino immigrant.
TIME AND PLACE	America now.
SITUATION	He is talking of his past, so could be played at any age. The piece is delivered like stand-up comedy.

Johnny: I've changed my parents' names to Fausto and Lala, to protect the innocent, namely me. I was born in Latin America, 'cause my moms was there, And when I was born, my moms was in labor for forty-eight hours, but she didn't care because she was enthralled with the miracle of creating life. 'Ow! Desgraciado, get this parasite out of me! Get it out of me now!! Coño.'

And my dad's going, 'If I had a nickel for every time I heard that.'

The doctor was also a little anxious, 'Push! Ms. Liquidzamo, Ms. Legs and amo, leg of lamb . . . Just push ma'am!'

'With what, cabrón! With what?!!'

And Dad says, 'I'm paying you, doctor! Why don't you pull!?'

'I am pulling! He's a stubborn little fuck.'

'Then leave him in there. Get up, woman, we're leaving.'

'But Fausto, he's half out.'

'So wear something loose. Come on, woman.'

So they walked out and my first view of the world was upside down and between my moms' legs. And they wonder why I have problems.

My parents left Latin America during the big plantain famine of the late sixties, and when they arrived in New York City they had such thick accents they couldn't even understand each other. My moms got all her English from watching television. 'Fausto, chock full of nuts is the heavenly coffee, they're creepy and they're cookie, that . . . that . . . that's all folks!'

'Woman, what the hell did you just say?'

'How should I know? I'm speaking English.'

At the airport, the nice, very white, very southern customs officer comes over to help. 'Come now, strip naked! Deep cavity search time. Last week we found five Nicaraguans inside one of you people.'

He starts searching my moms.

'OOhh, his hands are cold. Fausto, why don't you touch me like this?'

'Cause I'm not looking for anything, Hey, Mr. Officer, if we're being searched, why are you naked?'

'Shut up and bend over!'

He puts on a rubber glove and welcomes my dad to America.

'No, mister, please no! ow, ow, ow!' Then my dad started singing, 'America America God shed his grace on thee.'

The shuttle from the airport said 'Miserable and Huddled Masses' and my pops is like, 'This is our bus,' so we jumped on and ended up in the present-day Ellis Island – Jackson Heights, Queens. Our tenement building was like the modern Tower of Babel. When I walked through the streets I'd see every ethnicity under the sun. The Hindi guy would be like, 'You want curry candy? It burn the shit out of your buttocks. Ring of fire.' Then the Jamaican rasta, 'You people multiply like roaches go back, blood clots, batty fufu, chatty chatty. Tinga linga ling hear the money ring. Buyaca buyaca.' And the Korean newsstand guy, 'This is not a library, little punks. You buy magazine or kick your ass.'

My parents worked twenty-eight hours a day, fourteen days a week. I'm not bad at math; it's just that Latin people have to make the most of their time.

NOTES FOR THIS SPEECH:

'Desgraciado': displeased;

'Coño': Spanish version of the rudest four-letter word;

'cabrón': another vulgar Spanish expression, this time more male orientated;

'plantain': staple food, like a banana;

'fufu': African porridge;

'Buyaca buyaca': nonsense words in a reggae song.

Change any words if you feel that your audience would be confused or upset: **See Note 3**.

Make sure you do not play the whole thing on the same note or pace: **See Note 4**.

You are speaking to the audience: **See Note 6**.

A Latin-American accent is needed to match the lines; it is not important that your skin colour does: **See Note 7**.

9

THIS IS OUR YOUTH

Kenneth Lonergan

FIRST PERFORMANCES	New York 1996; London 2002
AWARDS	Nominated for the *Drama Desk Award for Outstanding New Play*.
CHARACTER	Dennis
PLAYED BY	Josh Hamilton; Mark Rosenthal [US]; Colin Hanks [UK]
CHARACTER'S AGE	21
CHARACTER'S TYPE	He is a charismatic student, who dabbles in drug dealing.
TIME AND PLACE	1982; New York apartment on the upper West Side.
SITUATION	Dennis is visiting his friend Warren, and trying to cope with life as a young adult. The carefree 1960s seem far away.

Dennis: Did my girlfriend call back?

Warren: No.

Dennis: I think I went too far with her before. But I can't even deal with it right now. I'm too freaked out. *[DENNIS lies down on his back.]* I just can't believe this, man, it's like so completely bizarre. And it's not like I even liked the guy that much, you know? I just *knew* him. You know? But if we had been doing those speedballs last night we could both be *dead* now. Do you understand how *close* that is? I mean . . . It's *death. Death.* It's so incredibly heavy, it's like so much heavier than like ninety-five percent of the shit you deal with in the average day that constitutes your supposed life, and it's like so totally off to the *side* it's like completely ridiculous. I mean that was *it*. That was his *life*. Period. The Life of Stuart. A fat Jew from Long Island with a grotesque accent who sold drugs and ate steak and did nothing of note like whatsoever. I don't know, man. I'm like, high on fear. I feel totally high on fear. I'm like – I don't even know what to *do* with myself. I wanna like go to *cooking* school in *Florence*, or like go into *show* business. I could so totally be a completely great chef it's like ridiculous. Or like an actor or like a director. I should totally direct movies, man, I'd be a genius at it. Like if you take the average person with the average sensibility or sense of humor or the way they look at the world and what thoughts they have or what they think, and you compare it to the way *I* look at shit and the shit I come up with to *say*, or just the *slant* I put on shit, there's just like no comparison at all. I could totally make movies, man, I would be like one of the greatest movie makers of all time. Plus I am like so much better at sports than anyone I know except Wally and those big black basketball players, man, but I totally played with those guys and completely earned their respect, and Wally was like, 'Denny, man, you are the only white friend I have who I can take uptown and hang out with my friends and not be *embarrassed*.' Because I just go up there and hang out with them and like get them so much more stoned than they've ever been in their *life* and like am completely not intimidated by them at *all*. You know?

NOTES FOR THIS SPEECH:

You may need to change the odd word or two: **See Note 3**.

The audience should find your conceit at being a potentially great chef or actor or director funny, and the more serious and convinced you are, the better it will be. And then you suddenly go off into being a great sportsman: **See Note 5**.

Although in the original he lies on the floor, for your purposes it might be better to use a chair: **See Note 8**.

10
THE PILLOWMAN
Martin McDonagh

FIRST PERFORMANCES	London 2003; New York 2005
AWARDS	**Won** the *Laurence Olivier Award for Best New Play*; nominated for the *Evening Standard Theatre Award for Best Play*, and the *Tony Award for Best Play*, and the *Drama Desk Award for Outstanding Play*.
	Billy Crudup nominated for the *Tony Award for Best Actor in a Play*.
	Jeff Goldblum [US: Tupolski] nominated for the *Drama Desk Award for Outstanding Featured Actor in a Play*.
CHARACTER	Katurian
PLAYED BY	David Tennant [UK]; Billy Crudup [US]
CHARACTER'S AGE	late 20s
CHARACTER'S TYPE	He is a sensitive writer, with a very twisted past.
TIME AND PLACE	Now and anywhere; the interrogation room.
SITUATION	Katurian is under interrogation by Tupolski, as there is a bizarre similarity between a series of gruesome murders and the plots of his stories. He has been told to read one of them that was published in a magazine.

Katurian: Um, 'Once upon a time in a tiny cobble-streeted town on the banks of the fast-flowing river, there lived a little boy who did not get along with the other children of the town; they picked on and bullied him because he was poor and his parents were drunkards and his clothes were rags and he walked around barefoot. The little boy, however, was of a happy and dreamy disposition, and he did not mind the taunts and the beatings and the unending solitude. He knew that he was kind-hearted and full of love and that someday someone somewhere would see this love inside him and repay him in kind. Then, one night, as he sat nursing his newest bruises at the foot of the wooden bridge that crossed the river and led out of town, he heard the approach of a horse and cart along the dark, cobbled street, and as it neared he saw that its driver was dressed in the darkest of robes, the black hood of which bathed his craggy face in shadow and sent a shiver of fear through the little boy's body. Putting his fear aside, the boy took out the small sandwich that was to be his supper that night and, just as the cart was about to pass onto and over the bridge, he offered it up to the hooded driver to see if he would like some. The cart stopped, the driver nodded, got down and sat beside the little boy for a while, sharing the sandwich and discussing this and that. The driver asked the boy why he was barefoot and ragged and all alone, and as the boy told the driver of his poor, hard life, he eyed the back of the driver's cart; it was piled high with small, empty animal cages, all foul-smelling and dirt-lined, and just as the boy was about to ask what kind of animals it was had been inside them, the driver stood up and announced that he had to be on his way. 'But before I go,' the driver whispered, 'because you have been so kindly to an old weary traveller in offering half of your already meagre portions, I would like to give you something now, the worth of which today you may not realise, but one day, when you are a little older, perhaps, I think you will truly value and thank me for. Now close your eyes.' And so the little boy did what he was told and closed his eyes, and from a secret inner pocket of his robes the driver pulled out a long, sharp and shiny meat cleaver, raised it high in the air and brought it scything down onto the boy's right foot, severing all five of his muddy little toes. And as the little boy sat there in gaping silent shock, staring blankly off into the distance at nothing in particular, the driver gathered up his bloody toes, tossed them away to the gaggle of rats that had begun to gather in the gutters, got back onto his cart, and quietly rode on over the bridge, leaving the boy, the rats, the river and the darkening town of Hamelin far behind him.'

Of *Hamelin*, see?

Tupolski: Of Hamelin.

Katurian: Do you get it? The little boy is the little crippled boy who can't keep up when the Pied Piper comes back to take all the children away. That's how he was crippled.

NOTES FOR THIS SPEECH:

In the story of *The Pied Piper of Hamelin*, all the children disappear, except the little crippled boy.

It will be easy for you to act the other person's speech: **See Note 1**.

It would be effective for you to act out the story, to make it as colourful and varied as possible: **See Note 4**.

Make the character of the driver as nice as possible, so that the shock of the ending is greater: **See Note 5**.

11

LOVE! VALOUR! COMPASSION!

Terrence McNally

FIRST PERFORMANCES	New York 1994; Manchester 1998
AWARDS	Won the *Tony Award for Best Play*, and the *Drama Desk Award for Outstanding Play*.
CHARACTER	Ramon
PLAYED BY	Randy Becker [US]; Danny Teeson [UK]
CHARACTER'S AGE	early 20s
CHARACTER'S TYPE	He is a flamboyant dancer.
TIME AND PLACE	Now; a beautiful Dutchess County farmhouse, 90 miles from New York.
SITUATION	Ex-dancer Gregory owns the property, and a group of his gay friends are sharing the weekend. His boyfriend Bobby has been casually seduced by Ramon, so Gregory is not pleased to see him swanning about the kitchen the next morning.

Ramon: Good morning, Gregory. The coffee's brewing, I woke up in my diva mode and there is no greater diva than Diana Ross. *[Sings a Diana Ross song.]* I figured you were working out there. I saw the lights. I didn't want to disturb you. How's it going. Don't ask, hunh? *[He sings a Diana Ross song and undulates. He's terrific.]* These are the exact movements that won me my high school talent contest. My big competition was a girl in glasses – Julia Cordoba – who played 'Carnival in Venice' on the trumpet. Next to 'You Can't Hurry Love' she didn't have a chance. But just in case anybody thought I was too good at Diana, I went into my tribute to Elvis, the title song from *Jailhouse Rock*. *[He sings from the title song from* Jailhouse Rock *and dances. He's electric. He remembers the choreography from the movie perfectly.]* I was turning the whole school on. Girls, boys, faculty. I loved it. If I ever get famous like you, Greg, and they ask me when I decided I wanted to be a dancer – no, a great dancer, like you were – I am going to answer, 'I remember the exact moment when. It was on the stage of the Immaculate Conception Catholic High School in Ponce in the Commonwealth of Puerto Rico when –' *[He slows down but keeps dancing.]* What's the matter? What are you looking at? You're making me feel weird. Come on, don't. You know me, I'm goofing. 'Great dancer you *are*.' I didn't mean it, okay? *[He dances slower and slower, but he has too much machismo to completely stop.]* Fuck you then. I'm sorry your work isn't going well. Bobby told me. But don't take it out on me. I'm just having fun. Sometimes I wonder why we bother, you know? Great art! I mean, who needs it? Who fucking needs it? We got Diana. We got Elvis. *[He has practically danced himself into GREGORY and is about to dance away from him at his original full, exuberant tempo when GREGORY grabs his wrist.]* Hey! *[GREGORY leads him to the sink.]* What are you doing? Let go. *[GREGORY throws a switch. We hear the low rumble of the disposal.]* What are you doing? I said. I don't like this. *[GREGORY turns off the disposal. He grabs RAMON'S other arm and twists it behind his back. At the same time he lets go of his wrist.]* Ow!

NOTES FOR THIS SPEECH:

You will not be able to include the business with the garbage disposal, which is included because we give you these pieces uncut.

You can sing and dance as much or as little as the occasion demands (this is a good speech to show off your other talents): See Note 2.

You can always cut the very last bit, or you may need to add a few words to indicate that he has grabbed you in a painful way (and you may want to tone down the strong language): See Note 3.

12

SIN (A CARDINAL DEPOSED)

Michael Murphy

FIRST PERFORMANCES	New York 2004
AWARDS	Nominated for the *Drama Desk Award for Outstanding Play*.
CHARACTER	Patrick McSorley
PLAYED BY	Pablo T. Schreiber
CHARACTER'S AGE	28
TYPE	He is the victim of priest abuse when a boy.
TIME AND PLACE	2002; Boston Court Room.
SITUATION	In the case against the Boston diocese, defended by Cardinal Law, a now-grown-up child victim finally gives his evidence about a paedophile priest, Father Geoghan. The narrator is Kreiger.

Patrick McSorley: My father committed suicide when I was six years old. The reason Father Geoghan had come to my mother's house was to give us his condolences – see, now, this was six years after my father's death . . . And he, uh, asked my mother if he could take me out for an ice cream. And you know, he was a priest. And to me – I grew up in a, you know, a lower class, you know, poor, you could say, neighborhood. And, um, I didn't, I didn't know Father Geoghan and at first it was, it seemed a little strange to me that a priest would just come by out of the blue that I didn't know, but he offered to take me out for an ice cream and I jumped at the chance because I was a poor kid and an ice cream was kind a big deal. On the way back, um, while we were in the car he, uh – this is really what gets me right here – it, it, you know, it still hurts and I get very angry when I think about it . . . Um. You know . . . I had shorts on, it was the summertime. And, uh, he asked, you know, you know, how's everything, how you doin' – in the middle of all that he started to tell me that he was sorry about my father's death, started to pat me on the leg. You know – sorry to hear about your father's death. Before I knew it his hands were up my shorts and he was grabbing at me. From what I could see, he had, there was something . . . He was going back and forth from the wheel to himself. And he had grabbed . . . I remember . . . I remember him grabbing napkins – and he gave one to me and kept the rest for himself. That's very sick. Uh, he, uh . . . We were driving on Brush Hill Road – he took the long way back. He, uh – I just remember him goin' real slow, goin' back and forth from the wheel to himself. And, uh . . .

Kreiger: Patrick McSorley died of a drug overdose a year after the conclusion of these proceedings. He was 29.

Patrick McSorley: Uh, I just remember – I was shocked, petrified. I couldn't talk. I couldn't move. My stomach was playing tricks on me. There was nothing I could do about it. You know, he must have sensed that I was very uncomfortable with what I, what he was doing, cause he, you know, he ended up slowly taking his hand out and getting me back to my house. But I just remember him getting out of the car and him asking me if I wanted him to make a return visit – and I was standing there on the sidewalk in front of my house with the ice cream all melted, all melted down my arm, and I just remember him smilin' at me as his car was driving off.

Before he took off, I remember him saying, let's just – just you and me. No one else has to know about this.

NOTES FOR THIS SPEECH:

There is a lot of hesitation in this speech: lots of 'um's' and 'uh's', making it natural and a 'real life' style of talking.

The speech by the Narrator might well be spoken by you: **See Note 1**.

This is a good speech to start really low and slow, and build to an emotional climax: **See Note 4**.

You are giving evidence, but could well talk to the audience: **See Note 6**.

13

AMADEUS

Peter Shaffer

FIRST PERFORMANCES	London 1979, 1998; New York 1980, 1999
AWARDS	Won the *Tony Award for Best Play*, and the *Drama Desk Award for Outstanding New Play*; nominated for the *Tony Award for Best Revival (Play)*.
	Simon Callow nominated for the *Laurence Olivier Award for Best Actor of the Year in a Supporting Role*.
	Tim Curry nominated for the *Tony Award for Best Actor*, and the *Drama Desk Award for Outstanding Actor in a Play*.
	Michael Sheen nominated for the *Laurence Olivier Award for Best Supporting Performance*.
CHARACTER	Mozart
PLAYED BY	Simon Callow, Michael Sheen [UK]; Tim Curry, Michael Sheen [US]
CHARACTER'S AGE	mid 20s
CHARACTER'S TYPE	He was the most famous musical prodigy of all time.
TIME AND PLACE	1780s; Vienna, the apartments of Salieri.
SITUATION	Mozart is scandalizing his fellow courtiers, the Court Composer Salieri, the Court Prefect Baron van Swieten, and the Court Chamberlain von Strack, with his ideas – but these also show his genius.

Mozart: I don't understand you! You're all up on perches, but it doesn't hide your arseholes! You don't give a shit about gods and heroes! If you are honest – each one of you – which of you isn't more at home with his hairdresser than Hercules? or Horatius? *[To SALIERI.]* Or your stupid *Danaius*, come to that! Or *mine* – mine too! *Mithridates, King of Pontus!* . . . *Il sogno di Scipione*! All those anguished antiques! They're all bores! Bores, bores, bores! *[Suddenly he springs up and jumps on to a chair, like an orator. Declaring it.]* All serious operas written this century are boring! . . . Well, nine hundred and ninety-nine out of a thousand! *[A pause. They turn and look at him in shocked amazement. He gives a little giggle, and then jumps down again.]*

Look at us! Four gaping mouths. What a perfect quartet! I'd love to write it – just this second of time, this *now*, as you are! *[Imitating their voices.]* Herr Chamberlain thinking: 'Impertinent Mozart. I must speak to the Emperor at once!' Herr Prefect thinking: 'Ignorant Mozart. Debasing opera with his vulgarity!' Herr Court Composer thinking: 'German Mozart. What can he finally know about music?' And Mozart himself, in the middle, thinking: 'I'm just a good fellow. Why do they all disapprove of me?' *[Excitedly to VAN SWIETEN.]* That's why opera is important, Baron. Because it's realer than any play! A dramatic poet would have to put all those thoughts down one after another to represent this second of time. The composer can put them all down at once – and still make us hear each one of them. Astonishing device: a vocal quartet! *[More and more excited.]* I tell you I want to write a finale lasting half an hour! A quartet becoming a quintet becoming a sextet becoming a septet – an octet – a nonet! On and on, wider and wider – all sounds multiplying and rising together – and the Together making a sound entirely new! . . . I bet you that's how God hears the world. Millions of sounds ascending at once and mixing in His ear to become an *unending music*, unimaginable to us! *[To SALIERI.]* That's our job! That's our *job*, we composers: to combine the inner minds of him and him and him, and her and her – the thoughts of chambermaids and court composers – and turn the audience into God. *[Pause. Embarrassed, MOZART sounds a fart noise and giggles.]*

I'm sorry. I talk nonsense all day: it's incurable – ask Stanzerl. *[To VAN SWIETEN.]* My tongue is stupid. My heart isn't.

'Hercules, Horatius, Danaius, Mithridates': characters from classical mythology;

'Stanzerl': another name for Mozart's wife Constanze.

Even though this character is known for his bad language, feel free to change particular words if that is best for your purposes: **See Note 3**.

Do not be afraid to go all out with this speech: you are meant to be an extreme character, with extreme ways of putting things, as long as you get the varieties in: **See Note 4**.

Take note of the last line, which indicates that you are aware of your outrageousness: **See Note 5**.

You will be able to place the other characters in a good position to give you a lot of variety; make sure the chair will take your weight: **See Note 8**.

14

PTERODACTYLS

Nicky Silver

FIRST PERFORMANCES	New York 1993
AWARDS	Nominated for the *Drama Desk Award for Outstanding Play*.
CHARACTER	Todd
PLAYED BY	T. Scott Cunningham
CHARACTER'S AGE	23
CHARACTER'S TYPE	He is an AIDS sufferer, with a lifelong interest in dinosaurs.
TIME AND PLACE	Now; USA – a lecture hall.
SITUATION	Todd is giving his first presentation on dinosaurs at a school lecture. Since this is a flashback, he could either be a schoolboy or his current age.

Todd: In the beginning, there were dinosaurs. Lots of dinosaurs. And they were big. They were very, very large – in comparison to man they were. They were huge. And there were many different kinds. There were ceratops and stegosauruses. There was the tyrannosaurus and the pterodactyl. And they lived, not in harmony, roaming the earth at will, raping, as it were, the planet and pillaging without regard, And, and um . . . uh . . . *[He loses his place and quickly checks his pockets for notes.]* Um, I seem to have forgotten my notes. I'm sorry. I thought I left them in my pocket. Maybe I wasn't supposed to wear this. Maybe I left them on the table. Maybe I – oh well, it doesn't matter now. I don't have them. That's the point. I think I remember most of it. – Maybe I left them – it doesn't matter.

Where was I? Oh, yes. It got cold. That's right, it got very, very cold and all the dinosaurs died. They all died. At once. It got cold and they died. And the land masses shifted and arranged themselves into the pattern we see now on the map. Basically. I think. There weren't any divisions for countries or states or anything, and I'm sure California was bigger, but it resembled what's on the map. During the cold spell, which is generally referred to as 'the ice age'- or maybe it was before the ice age, or after it – I can't remember – but life started spontaneously. In a lake. Here, I think. *[He indicates the Sea of Japan.]* And amoebas multiplied and became fish – don't ask me how – which evolved into monkeys. And then one day, the monkeys stood up, erect, realized they had opposing thumbs and developed speech. Thus, Mankind was born. Here. *[He indicates Africa.]*

Some people liked Africa, so they stayed there and became black. Some people left, looking for something, and became Europeans. And the Europeans forgot about the Africans and made countries and Queen Elizabeth executed her own half-sister Mary Queen of Scots. Some Europeans were Jewish, but most were Christians of some kind, Jesus having been born some time prior – oops, I forgot that. I'm sorry. Jesus was born. And there were other religions too, but I can't remember much about them, so I'm sure they weren't very important. During the Renaissance people got very fat. Picasso sculpted *David*, Marco Polo invented pizza, Columbus discovered the New World and Gaetan Dugas discovered the Fountain of Youth. Europeans imported tea, to drink, and Africans, to do their work. Edison invented the telephone. Martha Graham invented modern dance. Hitler invented fascism and Rose Kennedy invented nepotism. Orson Wells made *Citizen Kane* and mothers loved their children, who rebelled, when the sun shined most of the time, except when it rained and there was a rhythm to our breathing. There was an order to the world. And I was born here. *[He indicates Philadelphia.]* I give you this brief summary of events, this overview, so you'll have some perspective. I'm sure I got some of it wrong, I've lost my notes, but it's basically the idea. And I wanted you to have, I think, some sense of history.

NOTES FOR THIS SPEECH:

'David': sculpted by Michelangelo, about 400 years before Picasso's time;

'Marco Polo': famous fourteenth-century traveller;

'Gaetan Dugas': Patient Zero, the flight attendant rumoured to have been a major spreader of AIDS in the early days of the epidemic;

'Rose Kennedy': mother of President John Kennedy.

Since you will not have a real map, you can speak the names of where you are pointing. You can also place it where it is best for you to be seen: **See Notes 3 and 8**.

You start off at a young age, but can always get older as the story goes on, to give an adult conclusion to the piece: **See Note 4**.

15

LAUGHTER ON THE 23RD FLOOR

Neil Simon

FIRST PERFORMANCES	New York 1993; London 1996
AWARDS	Nominated for the *Laurence Olivier Award for Best Comedy*.
CHARACTER	Ira
PLAYED BY	Ron Orbach [US]; Linal Haft [UK]
CHARACTER'S AGE	20s
CHARACTER'S TYPE	He is a hypochondriac comedy writer, all energy with a touch of brilliant madness.
TIME AND PLACE	1953; The Writers Room at the offices of *The Max Prince Show*, New York.
SITUATION	Kenny is one of the writers, waiting for inspiration for their hit comedy TV show, when Ira enters, wearing a topcoat and scarf.

Ira: *[Holds his chest.]* I can't breathe, I can't catch my breath. I think it's a heart attack. It could be a stroke. Don't panic, just do what I tell you. *[He sits with his coat on. He talks breathlessly.]* Call Columbia Presbyterian Hospital. Ask for Dr. Milton Bruckman. Tell him I got a sharp stabbing pain down my left arm, across my chest, down my back into my left leg. If he's in surgery, call Dr. Frank Banzerini at St. John's Hospital, sixth floor, cardiology. Tell him I suddenly got this burning sensation in my stomach. At first I thought it was breakfast. I had smoked salmon. It was still smoking. It didn't feel right going down. If his line is busy, call the Clayton and Marcus Pharmacy on 72nd and Madison. Ask for Al. Tell him I need a refill on my prescription from Dr. Schneider. I can't remember the drug. Zodioprotozoc. No. Vasco something. Vasco da Dama, what the hell was it? I can't get air to my brain . . . This scarf is choking me, get it off my neck. *[He pulls it off, throws it away. No one has moved. They've all been through this before.]* Don't call my wife . . . No, maybe you should call her. But don't tell her it's a stroke. If she thinks it's a stroke, she'll call my mother. I have no time to talk to my mother, she drives me crazy. *[He begins to hyperventilate and wheeze, looking to the others who just stare.]* This could be it, I swear to God. *[He still wheezes, then looks at KENNY.]* Why are you just sitting there? What the hell are you waiting for?

Kenny: For you to die or finish your instructions, whichever comes first.

Ira: *[He gets up.]* You think this is a joke? You think this is funny? You think I would walk in here with a pain so bad, I – wait a minute! *[He holds his chest.]* Wait a minute! . . . Hold it! Wait a minute! *[He doesn't move.]* Ohhh. OHHH . . . I just passed gas! Thank God! I thought it was all over for me. Whoo.

NOTES FOR THIS SPEECH:

You can incorporate the other line into yours: See Note 1.

Make each instruction a different thought, with a different intensity: See Note 4.

You have two moments when the audience should think you are about to die: make the most of them: See Note 5.

16

TWILIGHT: LOS ANGELES, 1992

Anna Deavere Smith

FIRST PERFORMANCES	Los Angeles 1993; New York 1994
AWARDS	Nominated for the *Tony Award for Best Play*.
	Anna Deavere Smith nominated for the *Tony Award for Best Actress in a Play*.
CHARACTER	Michael
PLAYED BY	Anna Deavere Smith
CHARACTER'S AGE	20s
CHARACTER'S TYPE	The author performed all the different characters in this play as a one-woman show. This character is a representative of the Coalition Against Police Abuse.
TIME AND PLACE	1992; Los Angeles.
SITUATION	Michael reports what the police did to a fellow black citizen.

Michael:

I witnessed police abuse.

It was

about one o'clock in the morning

and, um,

I was asleep,

like

so many of the other neighbors,

and I hear this guy calling out for help.

So myself and other people came out in socks

and gowns

and, you know,

nightclothes

and we came out so quickly we saw the police had this brother

handcuffed

and they was beatin' the shit out of him!

You see,

Eugene Rivers was his name

and, uh,

we had our community center here

and they was doin' it right across the street from it.

So I went out there 'long with other people and we demanded they stop.

They tried to hide him by draggin' him away and we followed him

and told him they gonna stop.

They singled me out.

They began Macing the crowd, sayin' it was hostile.

They began

shootin' the Mace to get everybody back.

They singled me out.

I was handcuffed.

Um,

when I got Maced I moved back

but as I was goin' back I didn't go back to the center,

I ended up goin' around this . . .

it was a darkened

unlit area.

And when I finally got my vision

I said I ain't goin' this way with them police behind me,

so I turned back around, and when I did,

they Maced me again

and I went down on one knee

and all I could do was feel all these police stompin' on my back. *[He is smiling.]*

And I was thinkin' . . . I said

why, sure am glad they got them soft walkin' shoes on,

because when the patrolmen, you know, they have them

cushions,
so every stomp,
it wasn't a direct hard old . . .
yeah
type thing.
So
then they handcuffed me.
I said they . . .
well,
I can take this,
we'll deal with this tamarr [sic],
and they handcuffed me.
And then one of them lifted my
head up –
I was on my stomach –
he lifted me from behind
and hit me with a billy club
and struck me in the
side of the head,
which give me about forty stitches –
the straight billy club,
it wasn't a
P-28, the one with the side handle.
Now, I thought in my mind, said hunh,
they couldn't even knock me out,
they in trouble now.
You see what I'm sayin'?
'Cause I knew what we were gonna do,
'cause I dealt with police abuse
and I knew how to organize.
I say they couldn't even knock me out,
and so as I was layin' there
they was all standin' around me.
They still was Macing, the crowd was gettin' larger and larger and larger
and more police was comin'.
One these pigs stepped outta the crowd with his flashlight,

caught me right in my eye,

and you can still see the stitches *[He lowers his lid and shows it.]*

and

exploded the optic nerve to the brain,

ya see,

and boom *[He snaps his fingers.]*

that was it.

I couldn't see no more since then.

I mean, they . . .

they took me to the hospital

and the doctor said, 'Well, we can sew this eyelid up and these

stitches here

but

I don't think we can do nothin' for that eye.'

So when I got out I got a CAT scan,

you know,

and

they said,

'It's gone.'

So I still didn't understand it but I said

well,

I'm just gonna keep strugglin'.

We mobilized

to the point where we were able

to get two officers fired,

two officers had to go to trial,

and

the city on an eye

had to cough up one point two million dollars

and so

that's why

I am able to be here every day,

because that money's bein' used to further the struggle.

I ain't got no big Cadillac,

I ain't got no gold . . .

I ain't got no

expensive shoes or clothes.

What we do have

is an opportunity to keep struggling and to do research and to

organize.

NOTES FOR THIS SPEECH:

'Mace': tear gas;

'tamarr': the author recorded the interviews that make up the show, and this is what was on the tape.

If you speak this piece as it is written, and so take a tiny pause at the end of each line and nowhere else, it will give you a naturalistic delivery. The speech is laid out the way the author wrote it (and, yes, she did win an acting nomination for playing the many different roles in the play, including this male one).

You can shorten the speech to meet your needs: See Note 2.

A few word changes may be needed: See Note 3.

There is a change from the start to the end, as you grow in authority: See Note 4.

An Afro-American accent is needed to match the lines; it is not important that your skin colour does: See Note 7.

17

ARCADIA

Tom Stoppard

FIRST PERFORMANCES	London 1993; New York 1995
AWARDS	**Won** the *Evening Standard Theatre Award for Best Play*, **and** the *Laurence Olivier Award for Best New Play*; nominated for the *Tony Award for Best Play*; and for the *Drama Desk Award for Outstanding Play*.
CHARACTER	Valentine
PLAYED BY	Sam West [UK]; Robert Sean Leonard [US]
CHARACTER'S AGE	25 to 30
CHARACTER'S TYPE	A young mathematician.
TIME AND PLACE	The present day; Sidley Park, the ancestral home of the Coverlys in England.
SITUATION	Valentine, the eldest Coverly son, is in love with visiting author Hannah. She has asked him if he can come up with a mathematical formula to draw the picture of a leaf.

Valentine: If you knew the algorithm and fed it back say ten thousand times, each time there'd be a dot somewhere on the screen. You'd never know where to expect the next dot. But gradually you'd start to see this shape, because every dot will be inside the shape of this leaf. It wouldn't *be* a leaf, it would be a mathematical object. But yes. The unpredictable and the predetermined unfold together to make everything the way it is. It's how nature creates itself, on every scale, the snowflake and the snowstorm. It makes me so happy. To be at the beginning again, knowing almost nothing. People were talking about the end of physics. Relativity and quantum looked as if they were going to clean out the whole problem between them. A theory of everything. But they only explained the very big and the very small. The universe, the elementary particles. The ordinary-sized stuff which is our lives, the things people write poetry about – clouds – daffodils – waterfalls – and what happens in a cup of coffee when the cream goes in – these things are full of mystery, as mysterious to us as the heavens were to the Greeks. We're better at predicting events at the edge of the galaxy or inside the nucleus of an atom than whether it'll rain on auntie's garden party three Sundays from now. Because the problem turns out to be different. We can't even predict the next drip from a dripping tap when it gets irregular. Each drip sets up the conditions for the next, the smallest variation blows prediction apart, and the weather is unpredictable the same way, will always be unpredictable. When you push the numbers through the computer you can see it on the screen. The future is disorder. A door like this has cracked open five or six times since we got up on our hind legs. It's the best possible time to be alive, when almost everything you thought you knew is wrong.

NOTES FOR THIS SPEECH:

'algorithm': set of rules for solving problems, especially mathematical and scientific ones, solving things step-by-step and getting ever closer to the answer;

'Relativity and quantum': branches of physics that deal with the origins of everything.

You get more and more excited as the speech progresses: See Note 4.

Although it is set in England, any accent would do: See Note 7.

18

IT'S RALPH

Hugh Whitemore

FIRST PERFORMANCES	London 1981
AWARDS	Nominated for the *Laurence Olivier Award for Best Comedy*.
CHARACTER	Dave
PLAYED BY	Jonathan Linsley
CHARACTER'S AGE	20s
CHARACTER'S TYPE	He is a young man looking remarkably like Jesus Christ.
TIME AND PLACE	Today; a crumbling English country cottage.
SITUATION	Dave has been re-building the roof, with fatal results for the visitor Ralph, killed by the building collapsing. He is talking to Andrew, the owner of the cottage.

Dave: Poor old Ralph. I'd never seen anyone dead before. *[Pause.]*

Actually that's not true. There was someone. When I was a kid. My Dad's auntie. She was funny in the head. She thought she could flap her arms up and down and fly like a bird. They had her put away. But then, when she got older, Dad thought she should come and live with us. We had a house out in the country, in Essex. Dad thought she should end her days with the family and not in a loony bin. The house was very unusual. Tall and thin. And there was trees all round it. There was a gap in the trees, and through that gap you could see the Colchester to London railway line. My old aunt loved to watch the trains go by. They gave her a room on the top floor so she could see the trains clearly. They kept the window locked, just in case. One day she managed to prise the window open. She crawled onto the window-sill, flapped her arms up and down, and jumped. Poor old darling. Mum rushed out and found her. 'Don't look,' she said, but of course I did. Wasn't nasty or frightening. Just a funny bundle of clothes with legs and arms sticking out of it. Mum said it was a blessèd release. She often said that about people dying. *[Pause.]*

I suppose some people thought she killed herself because we kept her locked up and were cruel to her. Perhaps some people thought she was trying to escape and killed herself accidentally. Some people knew the truth, of course. And perhaps there was someone in a train going from Colchester to London. And perhaps he looked out of the window, and, perhaps, through that gap in the trees, he saw an old lady in mid-air, flapping her arms up and down. Just for a split-second, as the train rushed on, past our house. And he'd look through the window, that man, and he'd be amazed. He'd tell his friends, 'I saw an old lady flying.' he'd say. So in a way, it actually happened. What she wanted. Perhaps she died happy. What do you think?

NOTES FOR THIS SPEECH:

Be nice and happy for the pleasant parts of the speech, to give you a good gear change for the serious bits: **See Note 5**.

Place Andrew downstage of you: **See Note 8**.

19

JITNEY

August Wilson

FIRST PERFORMANCES	New York 2000; London 2001
AWARDS	**Won** the *Laurence Olivier Award for Best New Play*; nominated for the *Drama Desk Award for Outstanding New Play*.
CHARACTER	Shealy
PLAYED BY	Willis Burks II [US and UK]
CHARACTER'S AGE	20s
TYPE	A black numbers taker.
TIME AND PLACE	1977; a Pittsburgh gypsy cab station.
SITUATION	He is telling his friend Doub of his past failed romances, especially Rosie who he was obsessed with.

Shealy: Must be when he had that little yellow gal working for him. That's the only time you ever see me down there.

Doub: What ever happened to that gal?

Shealy: She married to one of them boys that drive a bus. That's what I hear.

Doub: She wasn't the one, huh?

Shealy: Naw she wasn't the one. I thought she was but then I believe Rosie done put a curse on me. She don't want me to have no other woman. But then she didn't want me. I told her baby, just tell me what kind of biscuits you want to make. I'm like the mill-man I can grind it up any way you want. She knew I was telling the truth too. She couldn't say nothing about that. She say you a poor man. What I need with a poor man? I told her say if I make a hundred I'll give you ninety-nine. She didn't trust me on that one but I went down to the crap game, hit six quick licks, left with a hundred and sixty-three dollars. I went on back up there. She let me in. I lay a hundred dollars down on the table and told her, 'Now, if I can just get one of them back I'd be satisfied.' She reached down and handed me a dollar and I went on in the room and went to bed. Got up and she had my breakfast on the table. It wasn't soon long that ninety-nine dollars ran out and next thing I knew she had barred the door. I went on and left but I never could get her off my mind. I said I was gonna find me another woman. But every time I get hold to one . . . time I lay down with them . . . I see Rosie's face. I told myself the first time I lay down with a woman and don't see her face then that be the one I'm gonna marry. That be my little test. Now with that little yellow gal used to work down at Pope's I seen Rosie's face . . . but it was blurry. Like a cloud or something come over it. I say, 'I got to try this again. Maybe next time I won't see nothing.'

She told me she didn't want to see me no more. She told me come back same time tomorrow and if she changed her mind she'd leave the key in the mailbox. I went up there and there was one man in the house and two others sitting on the doorstep. I don't know who had the key.

NOTES FOR THIS SPEECH:

A one act version of this play premiered in Pittsburgh in 1982.

'gypsy cab': taxicab that is licensed only to respond to calls but often cruises the streets for passengers.

You will need to let us know what Doub is saying to you: **See Note 1.**

The more you make us believe that you will succeed in staying with Rosie, the better the contrast will be with your disappointment: **See Note 5.**

An Afro-American accent is needed to match the lines; it is not important that your skin colour does: **See Note 7.**

20

ANGELS FALL

Lanford Wilson

FIRST PERFORMANCES	Miami, 1982; New York 1982
AWARDS	Nominated for the *Tony Award for Best Play*.
CHARACTER	Zappy
PLAYED BY	Brian Tarantina
CHARACTER'S AGE	21
CHARACTER'S TYPE	He is a professional tennis player; almost skinny; could be Latino.
TIME AND PLACE	Today; a small mission church in New Mexico.
SITUATION	A group of diverse people, including Vita and Doherty, are waiting in the church until the all-clear is given about a possible nuclear accident, and Zappy is telling them about his magic discovery.

Zappy: Or like when I found out I was a tennis player.

Vita: I love you.

Zappy: No, no joke. I went to church and lit a candle, man.

Doherty: You give thanks for that light.

Zappy: Really. I said my novenas, man, 'cause it had been like a – not a miracle that anyone would know except just me – but it had been like when those girls saw Our Lady of Fatima up on that hill. It was really weird. I was like in the fifth grade and I was watching these two hamburgers on some practice court, and they took a break and one of them hands me his racket. So I threw up a toss like I'd seen them do and zap! Three inches over the net, two inches inside the line. There wasn't nobody over there, but that was an ace, man. You should have heard those guys razz me. I mean, you know, they say, 'Man, you stink.' And all those things you can't repeat in front of a priest. They was really on my case. And I think that's the first time anybody ever looked at me. I mean, I was skinny, you've never seen – most of the girls in my homeroom had about twenty pounds on me. So this guy shows me a backhand grip and he hits one to me and zap! You mother! Backhand! Right down the line. And the thing is, that's where I wanted it. I saw the ball come at me, and I said I'm gonna backhand this sucker right down the line, and I did.

So then they took their ball back. Which I don't blame them, 'cause no high school hotshot is gonna get off on being showed up by this eleven-year-old creep that's built like a parking meter, you know?

But that was it. I hit that first ball and I said, 'This is me. This is what I do. What I do is tennis.' And once you know, then there's no way out. You've been showed something. Even if it's just tennis, you can't turn around and say you wasn't showed that.

So I went to church and said a novena for those meatballs 'cause they didn't know all the butterflies that was in my stomach, that they'd been my angels. But, man, on the way home, anybody had asked me what I did, right there I'd have said, 'I play tennis.' Didn't know love from lob, didn't matter. That's what I am. 'Cause once you know what you are, the rest is just work.

NOTES FOR THIS SPEECH:

'novenas': Catholic prayers, a series of nine days of prayers asking for something via the Virgin or a Saint.

The other characters' lines are easy to cope with: **See Note 1**.

The more you believe you will not be any good at tennis, the more you (and the audience) will be surprised when your very first ball is hit so well. You can then be very happy that your backhand went so well, in order to have a big gear change to show your disappointment when they then stopped playing with you: **See Note 5**.

Acting out the moves needed to play tennis will show off your physical prowess. You could always include a tennis racket: **See Note 9**.

21

METAMORPHOSES

Mary Zimmerman

FIRST PERFORMANCES	Chicago 1998; New York 2001
AWARDS	Won the *Drama Desk Award for Outstanding Play*; nominated for the *Tony Award for Best Play*.
CHARACTER	Phaeton
PLAYED BY	Doug Hara
CHARACTER'S AGE	late 20s
CHARACTER'S TYPE	He is a spoiled brat.
TIME AND PLACE	These are the stories from Ancient Greece, put into modern settings: today; a psychiatrist's office.
SITUATION	A patient tells his psychiatrist about his spoiled teenage years.

Phaeton: Well, my parents were separated when I was really little. Before I was even born. It was a sort of a one-night sort of thing – except it was in the day, in a meadow, where my mother went to watch my father pass by every day. Anyway, I always knew who he was, and I would see him pass by every day – of course – who doesn't? But I never knew him, and he wasn't really around. I mean, not *around* around.

I went to an expensive school and there were a lot of boys there who were, you know, sons of the rich and famous. And one day we're all on the playground and this one kid, Epaphus, he goes to me, 'So Phaeton blah blah who's your father, what does he do? Blah blah blah.' So I tell him my father's the sun and he says, 'Tell me another,' and I say 'He's the sun, he's Phoebus Apollo.' And he just basically trampled me, just basically beat the shit out of me. Like I was lying.

So I go home and I say, Mom this happened, you know at school. And she gets all upset, crying and everything, because she still loves him and it's an insult to her as well. And I'm like, well, if it's true how come there's no proof of it? It's unfair to us, you know, that there's no proof. And she gets more upset and she says: 'Hear me, my child. In all his glory, your father looks down upon us. By his splendor, I swear that you are his truly begotten son. That fiery orb you see crossing the sky each day whose heat enlivens and enables the world and orders our days and nights is indeed your sire. Believe me, my darling!' Blah, blah, blah.

So she tells me to go over to the valley where my dad goes to work every morning and just ask him to set things straight. To, you know, 'do right by me.' So I set out and it's hot and it's dusty and it's a long way – across Ethiopia. And I hitch part of the time and part of the time I walk and finally, *finally*, I get there. And the hill is steep.

At the door are my dad's secretaries, the days and the hours and the century, but they recognize me and they say go on in. And there he is all shining and golden, and I can't even look at him he's so bright. And you know what he says to me? He says, 'My son, you are welcome. Speak, Phaeton, to your father.' I cannot even tell you what this was to me. So I tell him everything, you know, I just spill my guts. He listens to me and he says, 'Let me grant you a favor, whatever you ask shall be yours.' And he swears to it.

Now, there's only one thing I want, I mean it's obvious, right? I say, 'Give me the keys to your car.' *Immediately*, he starts backpedalling, saying it's his job and no one else can do it, and that up in the sky there are the bull and the lion and the scorpion to get me, and I say, 'Give me the keys to your car. I want to drive it myself across the sky. It's my turn. You promised. I want to light the world today.'

Where have you been all my life, Dad? It's my turn. Hand it over! So he hands over the reins, but he won't stop giving advice. You know, like 'Don't fly too high, nor too low, stay in the tracks, go slantwise.' On and on. But I didn't listen.

It was over before it began. It was chaos, okay? Out of control, as if no one was driving. You know, my knees were weak, I was blind from all the light. I set the earth on fire. And I fell. And it just destroyed me – you know, I was just completely and utterly destroyed. O-V-E-R. Over.

NOTES FOR THIS SPEECH:

'sire': father.

The gaps are where the Therapist talks and comments to the audience, but you don't hear it. In the original production, Phaeton was floating in a swimming pool on an inflatable chair.

In the ancient Greek myth, Phaeton was the son of the sun god, called Helios, who drove his chariot (the sun) across the sky every day. Phaeton insisted on driving the chariot for one day, but it all went wrong and he left the earth burnt in some places, and too cold in others.

If you find it a bit long, you could drop some of the paragraphs; the first and last two?: See Note 2.

You may find that one or two words could well be changed: See Note 3.

Although you are talking to your psychiatrist, you can get up and move about as well: See Note 8.

30s

22

JOINED AT THE HEAD

Catherine Butterfield

FIRST PERFORMANCES	New York 1992
AWARDS	Nominated for the *Drama Desk Award for Outstanding New Play*.
CHARACTER	Jim
PLAYED BY	Kevin O'Rourke
CHARACTER'S AGE	38
CHARACTER'S TYPE	He is slightly overweight, slightly greying, and if he took care of himself he would be a good-looking man, but he hasn't.
TIME AND PLACE	Now; New York.
SITUATION	He and his wife Maggy are visited by his old flame, now a successful novelist. His wife is dying of cancer, and the visit forces him to confront realities. The Author specifically asks that the speech be more matter of fact than emotional.

Jim: [*His face goes from hopeful and encouraging to a mask of grief. He goes over to the water fountain. Washes his face as he drinks from it. Straightens up and looks at the audience.*] Here's what you won't hear from them about me. You won't hear about the nights I lie awake looking at Maggy, thinking about what a wonderful mother she would have made. Or how beautiful our children would have been. You won't hear about how I lust for her, even now, even with tubes running out of her body. How I fantasize about making her well with my ejac-ulations, as though it were a life-giving fluid that could wash through her entire body and render her clean again. Or about the other side of that, the self-hatred that goes along with forcing yourself upon a sick person. Even though she pretends it's voluntary, that she wants it, too. You won't hear about the anger, an anger so strong and vicious it feels like it could wipe out cities. Anger at the world, at fate, at this fucking roll of the dice that is your life. And anger at Maggy, for letting herself get so sick. For doing this to me and ruining my life. You particularly won't hear about this last because I don't tell it to anyone, least of all myself. You won't hear about my dreams, dreams of flight, of other women, of another life, the one with her we didn't get to have. You won't know what comfort I take in these dreams, the true happiness I find in them. And the strange sensation of waking up to discover that it's your life that is the nightmare, not the dream. 'Don't cry, Jim, it's only your life. You're asleep now, everything's okay.' You won't hear about the people I work with, and how they've reacted to all this. How some are compassionate and caring, and others treat me like I'm perhaps a carrier and they're going to get it themselves. Still others act as though nothing has happened, and I'm probably overreacting. And more than one woman is already shooting up flares – 'I'm available when all this is over!' Vulture women. If they knew my fantasies regarding them, every sphincter would open in abject fear. You won't hear about the effort it takes to stay positive, to keep hoping, to never let her know I've given up. And you won't know, because she couldn't possibly realize herself, how desperately and deeply I love her. My partner. My life partner. The one I'm joined to forever. My love. My wife. *[He takes another drink from the water fountain, slicks back his hair.]* I just thought you should know.

NOTES FOR THIS SPEECH:

Feel free to trim the speech (possibly the section about 'people I work with'), or to change words, to make the piece suitable for you: **See Notes 2 and 3**.

The author's suggestion that it be matter of fact was for a complete production; as an audition speech, you may find it useful to be more emotional: **See Notes 4 and 5**.

You are talking to the audience: **See Note 6**.

23

THREE DAYS OF RAIN

Richard Greenberg

FIRST PERFORMANCES	New York 1997; London 1999
AWARDS	Nominated for the *Drama Desk Award for Outstanding Play*, and the *Laurence Olivier Award for Best New Play*.
CHARACTER	Pip
PLAYED BY	Bradley Whitford [US]; David Morrissey [UK]
CHARACTER'S AGE	30s
CHARACTER'S TYPE	He is sunny, good-looking, almost helplessly happy.
TIME AND PLACE	Now; New York.
SITUATION	Old friends have met up, and compared their childhoods, and the nightmare of being a child. Pip is giving us his background.

[PIP rushes on, as though late, slams door behind him, catches his breath, smiles at audience.]

Pip: *[Solo.]* Hi. Hello. Okay: now me.

My name is Phillip O'Malley Wexler – well, Pip to those who've known me a little too long. My father, the architect Theodore Wexler, died of lung cancer at the age of thirty-eight, even though he was the only one of his generation who never smoked. I was three when it happened, so, of course, I forgot him instantly. My mother tried to make up for this by obsessively telling me stories about him, this kind of rolling epic that trailed me through life, but they, or *it*, ended up being mostly about her. Which was probably for the best.

Anyway, it went like this:

My mother, Maureen O'Malley back then, came to New York in the spring of '59. She was twenty, her parents staked her to a year, and she arrived with a carefully-thought-out plan to be amazing at something. Well, the year went by without much happening and she was miserable because she was afraid she was going to have to leave New York and return, in disgrace, to Brooklyn.

Early one morning, after a night when she couldn't sleep at all, she started wandering around the city. It was raining, she had her umbrella, she sat in the rain under her umbrella on a bench in Washington Square Park, and felt sorry for herself. Then she saw my father for the first time.

'There he was,' she told me, 'this devastatingly handsome man' – that was an exaggeration, he looked like me – and he was obviously, miraculously, even *more* unhappy than she was. He was just thrashing through the rain, pacing and thrashing, until, all at once, he stopped and sank onto the bench beside her. But not because of her. He didn't realize she was there. He didn't have an umbrella so my mother shifted hers over to him.

'Despair,' my mother told me, 'can be attractive in a young person. Despair in a young person can be seductive.'

Well, eventually she got tired of him not noticing the wonderful thing she was doing for him so she said, a little too loudly:

'Can I help you? May I be of help to you?'

Because he'd been crying.

And he jumped! Man, he *shrieked!*

But he stayed anyway, and they talked, and I was born, the end.

Okay. So, my mother had been telling me that story for about ten years before it occurred to me to ask: 'Why was he crying? What was my father so upset about the first time he met you?' 'I never knew,' she said. He just told her he was fine, she took him to breakfast, they talked about nothing, and I guess she kind of gawked at him. And the more she gawked, I guess the happier he felt, because by the end of breakfast it was as if nothing had happened and they were laughing and my mother was in love and the worst day of her life had become the best day of her life.

When she first came to New York, my mother would stay up till dawn debating Abstract Expressionism and *Krapp's Last Tape*, and then she'd sneak out to a matinee of one of those plays you could never remember the plot of where the girl got caught in the rain and had to put on the man's bathrobe and they sort of did a little dance around each other and fell in love. And there wasn't even a single good joke, but my mother would walk out after and the city seemed dizzy with this absolutely random happiness, and that's how she met my father.

She's hardly ever home anymore. She travels from city to city.

I think she's looking for another park bench, and another wet guy. That's okay. I hope she finds him.

NOTES FOR THIS SPEECH:

Krapp's Last Tape: abstract play by Samuel Beckett.

Find a different tone for the different sections of this speech: See Note 4.

You are talking to the audience: See Note 6.

24

THE NORMAL HEART

Larry Kramer

FIRST PERFORMANCES	New York 1985; London 1986
AWARDS	Nominated for the *Laurence Olivier Award for Best Play of the Year*.
	Martin Sheen [UK: Ned] nominated for the *Laurence Olivier Award for Best Actor*.
CHARACTER	Bruce
PLAYED BY	David Allen Brooks [US and UK]
CHARACTER'S AGE	late 30s
CHARACTER'S TYPE	He is gay, and exceptionally handsome.
TIME AND PLACE	1980s; Ned and Felix's apartment, New York.
SITUATION	Bruce's partner has died of AIDS at a time when people did not understand the condition properly, and no successful treatment had yet been found. He is visiting Ned, an activist in getting society to accept and understand what is happening in the gay community.

Bruce: He's been dead a week.

Ned: I didn't know he was so close.

Bruce: No one did. He wouldn't tell anyone. Do you know why? Because of me. Because he knows I'm so scared I'm some sort of carrier. This makes three people I've been with who are dead. I went to Emma and I begged her: please test me somehow, please tell me if I'm giving this to people. And she said she couldn't, there isn't any way they can find out anything because they still don't know what they're looking for. Albert, I think I loved him best of all, and he went so fast. His mother wanted him back in Phoenix before he died, this was last week when it was obvious, so I get permission from Emma and bundle him all up and take him to the plane in an ambulance. The pilot wouldn't take off and I refused to leave the plane – you would have been proud of me – so finally they get another pilot. Then, after we take off, Albert loses his mind, not recognizing me, not knowing where he is or that he's going home, and then, right there, on the plane, he becomes . . . incontinent. He starts doing it in his pants and all over the seat; shit, piss, everything. I pulled down my suitcase and yanked out whatever clothes were in there and I start mopping him up as best I can, and all these people are staring at us and moving away in droves and . . . I ram all these clothes back in the suitcase and I sit there holding his hand, saying, 'Albert, please, no more, hold it in, man, I beg you, just for us, for Bruce and Albert.' And when we got to Phoenix, there's a police van waiting for us and all the police are in complete protective rubber clothing, they looked like fucking astronauts, and by the time we got to the hospital where his mother had fixed up his room real nice, Albert was dead. *[NED starts toward him.]* Wait. It gets worse. The hospital doctors refused to examine him to put a cause of death on the death certificate, and without a death certificate the undertakers wouldn't take him away, and neither would the police. Finally, some orderly comes in and stuffs Albert in a heavy-duty Glad Bag and motions us with his finger to follow and he puts him out in the back alley with the garbage. He says, 'Hey, man. See what a big favor I've done for you, I got him out, I want fifty bucks.' I paid him and then his mother and I carried the bag to her car and we finally found a black undertaker who cremated him for a thousand dollars, no questions asked.

Would you and Felix mind if I spent the night on your sofa? Just one night. I don't want to go home.

NOTES FOR THIS SPEECH:

'Glad Bag': body bag.

It will be easy to act the missing line, and the stage instruction for Ned: **See Note 1**.

Change words if that suits your purposes: **See Note 3**.

Make sure it is not all on one gloomy note by finding the happiness in remembering Albert's love, and that they had to get another pilot. Also, the last line can be done very differently to the rest of the speech: **See Note 5**.

25

HAUPTMANN

John Logan

FIRST PERFORMANCES	Chicago 1987; New York 1992
AWARDS	Denis O'Hare nominated for the *Drama Desk Award for Outstanding Actor in a Play*.
CHARACTER	Hauptmann
PLAYED BY	Denis O'Hare
CHARACTER'S AGE	35
CHARACTER'S TYPE	He is a loner, and very intense.
TIME AND PLACE	1930s; a prison cell on Death Row.
SITUATION	Being questioned by two policemen, Hauptmann finally breaks, and gives a confession to the murder of Lindbergh's baby to the audience.

Hauptmann: Slowly he worked open the window with a chisel and reached one leg into the room and then the other. He was suddenly inside the house. He heard the sounds of people below and waited. As he waited he became aware of another sound. The soft . . . rhythmic . . . breathing . . . of . . . a baby.

He smiled as he listened to the warm sound. His hands sought the sound and discovered the crib, and inside the crib, the baby. Quickly he pulled the baby from the crib and placed the note on the window sill, he looked around the room one last time, gathering it all in. He felt the desire to laugh or sing or something. But silently he carefully stepped through the window onto the ladder. The baby was still asleep on his shoulder. Still the warm breathing continued, only a little louder in his ear.

And then – under his foot a rung snapped. Loudly the crack of wood echoed – he lost his balance and grabbed to stay on the ladder. In doing so the baby slipped from his arms. He made a mad grasp but missed by inches. Forever the baby seemed to tumble through the air. Finally, finally he saw the baby thud against the house and hit the ground. He died then.

The sound of the crack was loud and he climbed down the ladder quickly. He grabbed the ladder in one hand and snatched the baby into his arms. He tried to run across the lawn toward the car but the ladder and the baby were awkward and he felt warmth on his fingers – he thought of Colonel Lindbergh's fire. He dropped the ladder and looked down at the baby.

He finally reached the car and gently put the baby into the passenger seat and drove away. The baby slumped over in the seat and his blood was dark as it flowed across the seat. In panic he stopped the car, where he was not sure, and dragged the baby after him into the woods.

He found a clearing with a small ditch. Frantically he looked around. But of course it was only silent and cold and lonely. He knelt by the baby and looked at it. It grew paler and paler in the blue light. He looked and thought . . . they will want something, proof. Slowly he began to unbutton the sleeping suit.

Then he worked with his hands, strong hands, to cover the baby with leaves. He stood. And the Lindbergh baby lay dead at his feet.

NOTES FOR THIS SPEECH:

Acting out the speech will show off your mime and physical abilities.

If you cut the reference to 'Colonel Lindbergh's fire', it would make sure the audience did not know the famous event you are describing until the last few words, giving a great punch to the end: **See Note 5**.

This is a soliloquy, but with referring to yourself in the third person: **See Note 6**.

26

LOBBY HERO

Kenneth Lonergan

FIRST PERFORMANCES	New York 2001; London 2002
AWARDS	Nominated for the *Drama Desk Award for Outstanding Play*, and the *Laurence Olivier Award for Best New Comedy*. David Tennant [UK: Jeff] nominated for the *Laurence Olivier Award for Best Actor*.
CHARACTER	Bill
PLAYED BY	Tate Donovan [US]; Dominic Rowan [UK]
CHARACTER'S AGE	around 30
CHARACTER'S TYPE	He is a seasoned policeman, saddled with a junior female partner.
TIME AND PLACE	Now; the security officer's room in a New York apartment building.
SITUATION	Bill is talking to the security guard Jeff. He is worried that as his new partner is an attractive woman, his working relationship with her will be damaged if Jeff tells her about his private life.

Bill: You want me to tell you what *I* see out there?

Jeff: Sure.

Bill: I see a little girl wearin' a police uniform. OK? I see a little girl from the neighborhood who some moron told her she could be a cop. But she's not a cop right now. But if somebody takes a shot at her, or somebody else's life depends on her, they're not gonna know she's not a cop. They're gonna think she knows what she's doing. She walks around the corner where somebody's trying to rob somebody or rape somebody or kill somebody they're not gonna know she's a little girl in a cop suit, they're gonna see a badge and a uniform and a gun and they're gonna blow a hole through her fuckin' head. Somebody runs up to her and asks her to help 'em she's not gonna help 'em, she's gonna look around and say 'Where's Bill? Where's Bill?' – That's me: I'm Bill. Now, I could tell that girl likes me, it's only natural. I'm her partner, I'm a big strong father figure, whatever, gotta lot of experience, gotta lotta confidence, I'm know what I'm fuckin' doin' – and that's attractive to a woman, it's attractive to anybody. So she's attracted to me. That's OK. She's human. I'm human. But maybe part of what I'm doin', part of buildin' her confidence is makin' her feel like I'm interested in her too. Maybe that makes her feel impressive. Makes her feel cocky, makes her feel like she's got something on the ball. Makes her feel like she's really a cop. Now, do I need you tellin' her I'm upstairs havin' *sex* with somebody on my *shift* so she can think I'm some kind of fuckin' maniac who's just messin' with her head, so she can lose all her confidence in me and consequently all her confidence in herself? Because of your big fuckin' flappin' fuckin' mouth? And then go out and get herself killed? Or me? Or somebody else? This is not a game. We're not *door*men, We're *police*men. Yeah, I know, we're terrible and everything, but we're playing with our *lives* and the lives of the people we're supposed to protect. So I don't appreciate the fun I guess you're havin' at my expense, and more importantly at her expense, while you're sitting around here twiddling your fuckin' thumbs and waiting for, uh, William to come around and make his rounds so you can go to sleep. OK?

Jeff: Yeah.

Bill: You know what I really feel like doin'? I really feel like smacking the shit outta you. But I'm not gonna do that, because I don't do that. Just when I come around here in the future, just be aware that you don't know what I'm doing here, you have no idea, and keep your fuckin' nose outta my business. You understand me?

NOTES FOR THIS SPEECH:

It will be easy for you to act Jeff's lines: **See Note 1**.

Your circumstances may lead you to changing some words: **See Note 3**.

Find all the varieties you can in your build to the line 'go to sleep.': **See Notes 4 and 5**.

27

CELEBRATION

Harold Pinter

FIRST PERFORMANCES	London 2000; New York 2001, 2005
AWARDS	David Pittu nominated for the *Drama Desk Award for Outstanding Featured Actor in a Play*.
CHARACTER	Waiter
PLAYED BY	Danny Dyer [UK and US]; David Pittu [US]
CHARACTER'S AGE	20s to 30s
CHARACTER'S TYPE	He is a very talkative, name-dropping waiter.
TIME AND PLACE	Now; famous London restaurant.
SITUATION	During a meal between Suki and Russell, the waiter cannot keep his thoughts to himself.

Waiter: Do you mind if I interject?

Russell: Eh?

Waiter: I say, do you mind if I make an interjection?

Suki: We'd welcome it.

Waiter: It's just that I heard you talking about T. S. Eliot a little bit earlier this evening.

Suki: Oh you heard that, did you?

Waiter: I did. And I thought you might be interested to know that my grandfather knew T. S. Eliot quite well.

Suki: Really?

Waiter: I'm not claiming that he was a close friend of his. But he was a damn sight more than a nodding acquaintance. He knew them all in fact, Ezra Pound, W. H. Auden, C. Day Lewis, Louis MacNeice, Stephen Spender, George Barker,

Dylan Thomas and if you go back a few years he was a bit of a drinking companion of D. H. Lawrence, Joseph Conrad, Ford Madox Ford, W. B. Yeats, Aldous Huxley, Virginia Woolf and Thomas Hardy in his dotage. My grandfather was carving out a niche for himself in politics at the time. Some saw him as a future Chancellor of the Exchequer or at least First Lord of the Admiralty but he decided instead to command a battalion in the Spanish Civil War but as things turned out he spent most of his spare time in the United States where he was a very close pal of Ernest Hemingway – they used to play gin rummy together until the cows came home. But he was also boon compatriots with William Faulkner, Scott Fitzgerald, Upton Sinclair, John Dos Passos – you know – that whole vivid Chicago gang – not to mention John Steinbeck, Erskine Caldwell, Carson McCullers and other members of the old Deep South conglomerate. I mean – what I'm trying to say is – that as a man my grandfather was just about as all round as you can get. He was never without his pocket bible and he was a dab hand at pocket billiards. He stood four square in the centre of the intellectual and literary life of the tens, twenties and thirties. He was James Joyce's godmother.

NOTES FOR THIS SPEECH:

You need to establish where the diners are, and the lines they have to say: **See Notes 1 and 8**.

Build the speech to its illogical conclusion 'godmother': **See Note 4**.

All the people you mention are famous writers from different countries, and different times (so they could not have been in each other's company). Don't just make them a list, but give a different feeling and attitude to each one: **See Note 5**.

You can play this with any accent: **See Note 7**.

28

GLORIOUS!

Peter Quilter

FIRST PERFORMANCES	London 2005
AWARDS	Nominated for the *Laurence Olivier Award for Best New Comedy*.
CHARACTER	Cosme
PLAYED BY	William Oxbrow
CHARACTER'S AGE	early 30s
TYPE	He is a pianist, and accompanist to the worst singer in New York.
TIME AND PLACE	1944; Florence's apartment at the Hotel Seymour, New York.
SITUATION	Florence was famous as a non-singer convinced she was a prima donna. Cosme is describing Florence's final triumph at Carnegie Hall, including 'Clavelitos', her famous encore.

Cosme: Nobody else in that entire season at Carnegie Hall rivalled Madam's success. She was, you might say, an 'unqualified' triumph. The audience first had to prove their identity in order just to get inside, where they packed in as many as they could – people seemed to be hanging from the rafters. It was a record-breaking attendance. And everyone loved it. The atmosphere was electric. So lively that a stage hand simply moving a chair was greeted with screams and cries of 'Brava!' Everyone was just in that kind of mood. 'Clavelitos' was so popular that they demanded a reprise – requiring therefore that all the carnations and, indeed, the basket be returned to the stage. Three thousand people shouting

'Ole' has to be heard to be believed . . .! And there was laughter – endlessly. Noisy and abandoned. Though the regulars did their best to cover it with whistles and cheers. For Madam's selection of 'Old English Songs', she appeared – naturally – with her shepherdess gown and crook. Her entrance in the costume caused such a ruckus that we had to wait five full minutes before we could continue. Broadway composer Harold Arlen was seen during a selection of Russian songs – bent double, banging his head on the floor and yelling, 'I can't stand it, I can't stand it!' And the famed actress Tallulah Bankhead had to be dragged out of her box because she became completely hysterical. But as for the applause . . . my God – you'd never heard such applause. Never. Thundering and rapturous, drowning out the laughter as it always did. It was an incredible, joyous night – for her, for her friends, and for every single person in the audience. Every enthusiast that relished her, every ugly duckling that was inspired by her, every dreamer who looked up to her, and every cynical piano player that had grown to love her. *[Pause.]* . . . The only sadness – is that just one month after her greatest performance – Florence died . . . She did so in the same manner in which she lived – with a determined and confident smile on her face. She left behind no immediate relatives, so the Verdi Club inherited her estate – and her wings . . . I was with her in those final moments – and as I looked, I saw a truly contented expression. I am convinced that as she lay there, she was listening to her own soprano voice. Not that terrible sound that *we* all heard. But the voice that was in her head and in her heart . . . angelic . . . perfect . . . glorious . . .!

NOTES FOR THIS SPEECH:

For one of her costumes, Florence wore an outrageous pair of wings.

Starting off at a low level will give you a nice build to the end. It is important that you find all the varieties you can in the piece: See Note 4.

You are talking directly to the audience: See Note 6.

29

ART

Yasmina Reza, translated by Christopher Hampton

FIRST PERFORMANCES	Paris 1994; London 1996; New York 1998
AWARDS	Won the *Evening Standard Theatre Award for Best Comedy*, and the *Laurence Olivier Award for Best Comedy*, and the *Tony Award for Best Play*; nominated for the *Drama Desk Award for Outstanding Play*.
	Ken Stott nominated for the *Laurence Olivier Award for Best Actor*.
	Alfred Molina **won** the *Drama Desk Award for Outstanding Featured Actor in a Play*; nominated for the *Tony Award for Best Actor in a Play*.
CHARACTER	Yvan
PLAYED BY	Pierre Arditi [France]; Ken Stott [UK]; Alfred Molina [US]
CHARACTER'S AGE	30 onwards
CHARACTER'S TYPE	He is a failed businessman about to get married. Could be any age from 30 to 50.
TIME AND PLACE	Now; an expensive apartment in Paris (but could be anywhere).
SITUATION	Two friends, Sege and Marc, are arguing over whether a completely white canvas is art, when Yvan arrives with news of his upcoming marriage to Catherine, talking as he enters.

Yvan: So, a crisis, insoluble problem, major crisis, both step-mothers want their names on the wedding invitation. Catherine adores her step-mother, who more or less brought her up, she wants her name on the invitation, she wants it and her step-mother is not anticipating, which is understandable, since the mother is dead, not appearing next to Catherine's father, whereas my step-mother, whom I detest, it's out of the question her name should appear on the invitation, but my father won't have his name on it if hers isn't, unless Catherine's step-mother's is left off, which is completely unacceptable, I suggested none of the parents' names should be on it, after all we're not adolescents, we can announce our wedding and invite people ourselves, so Catherine screamed her head off, arguing that would be a slap in the face for her parents who were paying through the nose for the reception, and particularly for her step-mother, who's gone to so much trouble when she isn't even her daughter and I finally let myself be persuaded, totally against my better judgement, because she wore me down, I finally agreed that my step-mother, whom I detest, who's a complete bitch, will have her name on the invitation, so I telephoned my mother to warn her, mother, I said, I've done everything I can to avoid this, but we have absolutely no choice, Yvonne's name has to be on the invitation, she said, if Yvonne's name is on the invitation, take mine off it, mother, I said, please, I beg you, don't make things even more difficult, and she said, how dare you suggest my name is left to float around the card on its own, as if I was some abandoned woman, below Yvonne, who'll be clamped on to your father's surname, like a limpet, I said to her, mother, I have friends waiting for me, I'm going to hang up and we'll discuss all this tomorrow after a good night's sleep, she said, why is it I'm always an afterthought, what are you talking about, mother, you're not always an after-thought, of course I am and when you say don't make things even more difficult, what you mean is, everything's already been decided, everything's been organised without me, everything's been cooked up behind my back, good old Huguette, she'll agree to anything and all this, she said – to put the old tin lid on it – in aid of an event, the importance of which I'm having some trouble grasping, mother, I have friends waiting for me, that's right, there's always something better to do, anything's more important than I am, good-bye and she hung up.

In order to give variety to the barrage of words, it would be nice to give very different characters, and perhaps voices, to the various people in your story: **See Notes 4 and 7**.

You will need to establish where the others characters are as you issue this stream of words: **See Note 8**.

30

THE KENTUCKY CYCLE

Robert Schenkkan

FIRST PERFORMANCES	Washington 1991; New York 1993
AWARDS	Won *The Pulitzer Prize for Drama*; nominated for the *Tony Award for Best Play*, and the *Drama Desk Award for Outstanding Play*.
	Stacy Keach nominated for the *Drama Desk Award for Outstanding Actor in a Play*.
CHARACTER	Michael
PLAYED BY	Stacy Keach
CHARACTER'S AGE	35
CHARACTER'S TYPE	He is a pioneer, an immigrant from Ireland.
TIME AND PLACE	Late 1700s; a cabin in Kentucky.
SITUATION	He has seen his wife and children killed by the local Indians, and now realises he needs another family.

Michael: I been killin' as long as I can remember. Ireland. Georgia. Here. Never for the pleasure innit, ya understand – though I'm good at it, and a man should take pride in what he does well. But if you go simple with blood you can lose your way. And I meant never to do that. I was always headed somewheres better. I killed my first man when I was seven. A bloody lobsterback. One o' them that was runnin' our piece of Ireland like his own bloody vegetable patch. They'd have 'hunts' on the land, see. Our land. Racin' through our fields on their fine horses in their blacks and scarlets. A beautiful sight! If you could just forget it was your crops out there bein' trampled underfoot for their sport. *[Beat.]*

Did you ever notice how like the distant bayin' of a fine pack of hounds is the sound of a hungry child cryin' hisself to sleep? *[Beat.]*

One of the silly bastards had too much to drink and lagged behind the rest. He failed to clear a wall and took a bad fall. His horse rolled over him. Must've broke him all up inside, 'cause he couldn't move none. I got to him first. I stood there, over him, and I remember him lookin' up at me with the queerest look on his face. What a sight I must've been: little snot-nosed, barefoot boy, more dirt than clothes. I wondered what he thought now; him and his kind always bein' so high and mighty. And then I stepped on his neck and broke it. Like St. Patrick crushin' a snake. *[Beat.]*

But there was no sport innit. See, I learned early, blood's just the coin of the realm, and it's important to keep strict accounts and pay your debts. That's all. And now here, at last, I'm a man of property meself, on the kind of land ya only dream about. Dirt so rich I could eat it with a spoon. I've but to piss on the ground and somethin' grows. I've corn for whiskey and white oaks for barrels to put it in and a river to float it down and sell it. I've everythin' I've ever wanted: the land, and to be left alone on it. I'm richer than that snotnosed boy ever dreamed he'd be. But somethin' isn't right. *[Beat.]*

I'm gettin' in and layin' by more food than one man could eat in a year. And instead of feelin' full, I feel empty. I feel *hungry*. What's the point, after so much blood and so much sweat, if ten years after I'm gone, the damn forest covers my fields again? Or worse, some *stranger* does? Will I have built all of this for nothin'? For no *one*? Michael, me boy, what you want is a family. And for that, you need a *wife*.

NOTES FOR THIS SPEECH:

'lobsterback': British soldier during the American revolution (a Redcoat).

The tougher you are describing your life, the softer you can be on wanting a wife: **See Note 5**.

You are telling the audience how you feel: **See Note 6**.

You could do this with either an Irish or American accent: **See Note 7**.

31

AMADEUS

Peter Shaffer

FIRST PERFORMANCES	London 1979, 1998, New York 1980, 1999
AWARDS	Won the *Tony Award for Best Play*, and the *Drama Desk Award for Outstanding New Play*; nominated for the *Tony Award for Best Revival (Play)*.
	Paul Scofield nominated for the *Laurence Olivier Award for Best Actor of the Year in a New Play*.
	Ian McKellen won the *Tony Award for Best Actor in a Play*, and the *Drama Desk Award for Outstanding Actor in a Play*.
	David Suchet nominated for the *Laurence Olivier Award for Best Actor*, the *Evening Standard Theatre Award for Best Actor*, and the *Tony Award for Best Actor*.
CHARACTER	Salieri
PLAYED BY	Paul Scofield, David Suchet [UK]; Ian McKellen, David Suchet [US]
CHARACTER'S AGE	31
CHARACTER'S TYPE	He has a mediocre talent, but has dedicated himself to God in order to be a great musician. Because he is remembering, he could be played at any age.
TIME AND PLACE	1823; in Salieri's apartments in Vienna.
SITUATION	Salieri was the Court Composer when the great musical genius Mozart arrived. Mozart's coarse behaviour and language upset all Salieri's plans, and philosophy. He talks to the audience of his memory of the first time he heard Mozart's music.

Salieri: And then, right away, the concert began. I heard it through the door – some serenade: at first only vaguely – too horrified to attend. But presently the sound insisted – a solemn Adagio, in E Flat.

It started simply enough: just a pulse in the lowest registers – bassoons and basset horns – like a rusty squeezebox. It would have been comic except for the slowness, which gave it instead a sort of serenity. And then suddenly, high above it, sounded a single note on the oboe.

It hung there unwavering, piercing me through, till breath could hold it no longer, and a clarinet withdrew it out of me, and sweetened it into a phrase of such delight it had me trembling. The light flickered in the room. My eyes clouded! *[With ever-increasing emotion and vigour.]* The squeezebox groaned louder, and over it the higher instruments wailed and warbled, throwing lines of sound around me – long lines of pain around and through me – Ah, the pain! Pain as I had never known it. I called up to my sharp old God *'What is this? . . . What?'* But the squeezebox went on and on, and the pain cut deeper into my shaking head, until suddenly I was running – dashing through the side-door, stumbling downstairs into the street, into the cold night, gasping for life. *[Calling up in agony.]* *'What?! What is this? Tell me, Signore!* What is this *pain?* What is this *need* in the sound? Forever unfulfillable yet fulfilling him who hears it, utterly. Is it *Your* need? Can it be Yours?' . . . *[Pause.]*

Dimly the music sounded from the salon above. Dimly the stars shone on the empty street. I was suddenly frightened. It seemed to me that I had heard the voice of God – and that it issued from a creature whose own voice I had also heard – and it was the voice of an obscene child!

NOTES FOR THIS SPEECH:

Make sure you start the speech at quite a low level, so as to give yourself somewhere to go for the finale: See Note 4.

The last few words should be a surprise for the audience: See Note 5.

This is a soliloquy: See Note 6.

32

DOUBT, A PARABLE

John Patrick Shanley

FIRST PERFORMANCES	New York 2004; Dublin 2006
AWARDS	Won *The Pulitzer Prize for Drama*, and the *Tony Award for Best Play*, and the *Drama Desk Award for Outstanding Play*.
	Brian F. O'Byrne won the *Drama Desk Award for Outstanding Actor in a Play*; nominated for the *Tony Award for Best Actor in a Play*.
CHARACTER	Father Flynn
PLAYED BY	Brian F. O'Byrne [US]; Aidan Kelly [Ireland]
CHARACTER'S AGE	late 30s
CHARACTER'S TYPE	He is a working-class priest, from the Northeast.
TIME AND PLACE	1964; a Catholic church in the Bronx, New York.
SITUATION	Dressed in blue and white vestments, he is giving a sermon, the topic being a reflection of the rumours going around the parish about him and children.

Father Flynn: A woman was gossiping with a friend about a man she hardly knew – I know none of you have ever done this – and that night she had a dream. A great hand appeared over her and pointed down at her. She was immediately seized with an overwhelming sense of guilt. The next day she went to confession. She got the old parish priest, Father O'Rouke, and she told him the whole thing. 'Is gossiping a sin?' she asked the old man. 'Was that the Hand of God Almighty pointing a finger at me? Should I be asking your absolution? Father, tell me, have I done something wrong?' *[Irish brogue.]* 'Yes!' Father O'Rouke answered her.

'Yes, you ignorant, badly brought-up female! You have borne false witness against your neighbor, you have played fast and loose with his reputation, and you should be heartily ashamed!' So the woman said she was sorry and asked forgiveness. 'Not so fast!' says O'Rouke. 'I want you to go home, take a pillow up on your roof, cut it open with a knife, and return here to me!' So she went home, took the pillow off her bed, a knife from the drawer, went up the fire escape to the roof, and stabbed the pillow. Then she went back to the old priest as instructed. 'Did you gut the pillow with the knife?' he says. 'Yes, Father.' 'And what was the result?' 'Feathers,' she said. 'Feathers?' he repeated, 'Feathers everywhere, Father!' 'Now I want you to go back and gather up every last feather that flew out on the wind!' 'Well,' she says, 'it can't be done. I don't know where they went. The wind took them all over.' 'And that,' said Father O'Rouke, 'is *gossip*!' In the name of the Father, Son, and the Holy Ghost, Amen.

NOTES FOR THIS SPEECH:

Getting humour and laughs with the speech will make the serious ending even more effective. Having made the point, you unexpectedly end the sermon: **See Note 5**.

You are addressing the audience as if they are your congregation: **See Note 6**.

There is no evidence that Father Flynn is a good actor, so the Irish brogue or accent does not have to be accurate: **See Note 7**.

33

BUICKS

Julian Sheppard

FIRST PERFORMANCES	New York 2003
AWARDS	Nominated for the *Drama Desk Award for Outstanding Play*.
	Norbert Leo Butz nominated for the *Drama Desk Award for Outstanding Actor in a Play*.
CHARACTER	Bill
PLAYED BY	Norbert Leo Butz
CHARACTER'S AGE	35
CHARACTER'S TYPE	He is a car salesman, whose wife has left him.
TIME AND PLACE	Today; motel room near Albuquerque.
SITUATION	Bill has taken his Mexican receptionist with him as he looks for his wife. He is in a motel room, explaining to her his situation.

Bill: My wife left me.

Naranja: I am sorry, what? At a funeral?

Bill: I came home to a note. She left me and I don't know where she went. She should have come here. I thought she'd come here. Things aren't as they're supposed to be. Nothing is as it's supposed to be. Do you understand that?

Naranja: Yes.

Bill: What am I supposed to do now? My wife *left* me . . . I have a wife. I got married. I got her pregnant and married her. We had been dating three months before we moved in together. She was my first real girlfriend ever. I never had that moment where I just stopped and looked at her and said 'I love this woman. I love her so much.' Not even when she told me she was pregnant and I said I would marry her. It was all just what I had to do. God, maybe it's good she went away, that I won't have her to – kick around anymore. Just her being there reminded me that I had a life before this. Well, maybe not a life, I never really had a life, but the *illusion* that I had a life. It's like it all just happened. Her, and the kids, and . . . Danny's better than me. And he knows it, my *child*, that he's better than me. Sometimes he looks at me and I can just see him thinking . . . 'What a dork. What a *loser.*' Maybe I don't want to be around *that*, maybe I'm grateful I won't have to feel like an asshole every time my son is in the room. And even if I found her, what would I say to her? 'I love you'? That wouldn't mean anything. Be just one more lie. And she would know it. She's known I was a liar for years.

Naranja: Mr Abeline –

Bill: Just why'd she take my kids? Like I don't even deserve them. Is she right? Am I, am I contagious? Am I so awful that if she didn't take them away from me I ruin them forever? Does she think I don't love them? Is that – oh, god, maybe I could ruin them, look at what I've done, I'm sorry, I'm sorry I dragged you here, this is practically kidnapping, across state lines, you could have me thrown in jail and my case would suck, they could throw me in jail forever and they'd basically be right –

Naranja: You have not kidnapped me. I am sorry about your wife. I am sorry about your children. This is terrible thing.

Bill: I can't be that bad, can I? I'm a good guy, right? I'm still a good guy. People, people like me . . .

NOTES FOR THIS SPEECH:

'dork': dull stupid person.

Naranja, your receptionist, has a few speeches: See Note 1.

Make sure each paragraph has a different approach, that you make a change in your attitude: See Note 4.

Make sure she is placed downstage of you: See Note 8.

34

RAISED IN CAPTIVITY

Nicky Silver

FIRST PERFORMANCES	New York 1995
AWARDS	Nominated for the *Drama Desk Award for Outstanding Play*.
CHARACTER	Sebastian
PLAYED BY	Peter Frechette
CHARACTER'S AGE	early 30s
CHARACTER'S TYPE	He is a *Vanity Fair* writer, now unemployed due to using unsourced material.
TIME AND PLACE	Now; a therapist's office in New York.
SITUATION	Sebastian has re-met his twin sister Bernadette at his mother's funeral, and decided to liven up and end his therapy. His therapist is seated at a desk, and he is seated opposite her. He is quite anxious.

Sebastian: I don't know how to say this. I, I'm not sure how to approach it. Um. The thing is, the thing is I've made a decision. I have. *[He shifts in his chair.]* I've been coming here, to see you, every Friday for four and a half years. It's become a habit, something I do without questioning. But this morning my mother was buried – did I mention that? She was. She died. She was killed by her shower-massage. Anyway, there, at her funeral, certain things became disturbingly clear to me. My sister was there. She sang. As you know, I've mentioned Bernadette, I think she's completely insane. For instance, our birthday parties were pageants of hysteria. My mother always gave us one party, our being twins, and every year Bernadette would have what I recognized, even then, as mini-nervous breakdowns. When we were ten, we had a clown. I'll never forget it. That was the year, I think, she slipped, irredeemably, 'round the bend.

It was hot, August, and the temperature must've reached a hundred and ten in that front yard. There were about two dozen children there, none of whom I particularly liked, and none of whom was having a particularly good time. We just sat there, sad, withered children on a patch of brown, burned-up grass. My mother had, as always, planned every moment of the day with military precision. Two o'clock: three-legged races. Two fifteen: passing oranges under our chins. At three o'clock, the entertainment arrived. A clown: Mr. Giggles. Mr. Giggles was *extremely* old. It's true that all adults seem old to small children, but Mr. Giggles would have seemed *very old* to very old people! He was old. His skin was the texture and non-color of white raisins.

In any event, Mr. Giggles made flowers spring from umbrellas and foam balls appear from behind our ears. He was maniacally cheerful, despite the fact that none of us joined in or laughed or moved. Mr. Giggles thought some singing might rouse us from our collective coma. He sang 'A Hundred Bottles of Beer on the Wall.' Only we were ten, so he sang 'A Hundred Bottles of *Milk* on the Wall.' Not very imaginative was Mr. Giggles. He sang loudly and with what should have been infectious joy: 'A hundred bottles of milk on the wall, a hundred bottles of milk!' And we tried! We did. At first. All of us, I think, joined in, Mr. Giggles ran around in a desperate frenzy, wild for us to perform – but it was so hot! We made it through ninety bottles of milk on the wall and eighty bottles of milk. And then . . . I could take it no more. I just stopped. I lay down, put my head on the earth and shut my eyes. Well, Mr. Giggles ran over and knelt down and sang *right* at me, loud, shouting more than singing really. Screaming right at me: 'EIGHTY- TWO BOTTLES OF MILK ON THE WALL! EIGHTY-TWO BOTTLES OF MILK!' I refused to stir. I just opened my eyes and stared at this *fascist* clown. Then another little boy stopped. Tommy Leonardo, I think. He let his head fall forward and fell silent. Giggles leapt upon him and shrieked with rage, 'EIGHTY-ONE BOTTLES OF MILK ON THE WALL! EIGHTY-ONE BOTTLES OF MILK!' Then very quickly, other children followed suit. Like spontaneous suicides, their voices fell silent. By now Mr. Giggles was in the throes of a demented fit! Running crazily from child to child, screaming, spit flying out of him, sweat spraying off of him. – But he would not give up! By now, no one was singing, except for my sister, who would participate in this deranged duet at any cost! I watched as Giggles flapped his arms like spastic birds and lost the count completely: 'FIFTY-TWO BOTTLES OF

91

MILK ON THE WALL! FORTY-EIGHT BOTTLES OF MILK!' And then he fell over in a sad, wet, broken-pencil heap. *[Pause.]*

The silence was palpable. My sister, abandoned, looked at me. 'He's dead,' I whispered. Bernadette shrieked and ran in horror from the yard and into the street, where a bread truck swerved to avoid her and ran headlong into a mammoth oak tree, shaking from its perch our cat, which fell to an ugly, bloody death, impaled by the truck's antenna and splattered on the windshield.

NOTES FOR THIS SPEECH:

Vanity Fair: American magazine of culture, fashion, and politics.

It would be fun to give an old man voice and movements to your imitation of Mr. Giggles.

If this is too long for your purposes, you could drop the first paragraph, and perhaps the last paragraph if that suited your purposes: See Note 2.

The end should be a complete surprise to us all: See Note 5.

35

KING HEDLEY II

August Wilson

FIRST PERFORMANCES	Pittsburgh 1999; New York 2001; London 2002
AWARDS	Nominated for the *Tony Award for Best Play*.
	Brian Stokes Mitchell nominated for the *Tony Award for Best Actor in a Play*, and the *Drama Desk Award for Outstanding Actor in a Play*.
CHARACTER	King
PLAYED BY	Tony Todd; Brian Stokes Mitchell [US]; Nicholas Monu [UK]
CHARACTER'S AGE	30s
CHARACTER'S TYPE	He has a vicious scar running down his face. He spent seven years in prison, and strives to live by his own moral code.
TIME AND PLACE	1985; Pittsburgh, backyards of houses in the Hill District.
SITUATION	King is explaining to Elmore how he got his scar. Elmore has just killed Leroy.

King: I don't know about you and Leroy but Pernell made me kill him. Pernell called me 'champ.' I told him my name's King. He say, 'Yeah, champ.' I go on. I don't say nothing. I told myself 'He don't know.' He don't know my daddy killed a man for calling him out of his name. He don't know he fucking with King Hedley II. I got the atomic bomb as far as he's concerned. And I got to use it. They say God looks after fools and drunks. I used to think that was true. But seeing as how he was both . . . I don't know anymore. He called me 'champ' and I didn't say nothing. I put him on probation. Told myself he don't know but I'm gonna give him a chance to find out. If he find out and come and tell me he's sorry then I'll let him live. I'm gonna fuck him up. I'm gonna bust both his kneecaps. But I'm gonna let him live. Saturday. I don't know why it's always on a Saturday. Saturday I went up to buy me some potatoes. I say, 'I want to have some mashed potatoes.' I told Neesi, say, 'You get the milk and butter and I'll get the potatoes.' I went right up there to Hester's on Wylie. I went up there and got me ten pound of potatoes. I started to get twenty but they only had one bag and it was tore, the bag was tore. I didn't want them to spill out on the way home. If I had been carrying twenty pounds of potatoes maybe I would have went home a shorter way. I say, 'Let me breeze by Center Avenue on my way home and let me see if I see Charlie. He owe me twenty dollars and if he pay me that might bring me some luck.' I got halfway down there and I seen Pernell. First thing I tell myself is, 'I ain't gonna be nobody's champ today.' I fix that hard in my head and I try to walk past him. I didn't want to ignore him so I say, 'How you doing, Pernell?' I don't really care how he doing. I'm just being polite like Mama Louise taught me. No sooner than the words got out my mouth then I felt something hot on my face. A hot flash and then something warm and wet. This nigger done cut me! He hit me with that razor and I froze. I didn't know what happened. It was like somebody turned on a light and it seem like everything stood still and I could see him smiling. Then he ran. I didn't know which way he ran. I was still blinded by that light. It took the doctor four hours and a hundred and twelve stitches to sew me up. I say, 'That's all right, the King is still here.' But I figure that scar got to mean something. I can't take it off. It's part of me now. I figure it's got to mean something. As long as Pernell was still walking around it wasn't nothing but a scar. I had to give it some meaning.

It wasn't but two weeks later and I'm thinking about this thing. I'm thinking what it gonna mean to everybody. I thought about his mama. I thought the whole thing out. It ain't easy to take somebody's life. I told myself 'It's me or him,' even though I knew that was a lie. I saw his funeral. I heard the preacher. I saw the undertaker. I saw the gravediggers. I saw the flowers. And then I see his woman. That's the hardest part. She know him better than anybody. She know what makes him bleed. She know why he breathes, what he sound like when he wakes up in the morning. She know when he's hungry and what will satisfy him. She know everything what nobody else don't know. It was hard but I told myself she got to suffer. She got to play the widow. She got to cry the tears.

About two weeks later I saw Pernell going into Irv's bar. He went straight back to the phone booth. I don't know who he was calling but that was the last call he made. I saw my scar in the window of the phone booth. I tapped on the glass. He turned and looked and froze right there. The first bullet hit him in the mouth. I don't know where the other fourteen went. The only regret is I didn't get away. I didn't get away with murder that time. You always regret the one you don't get away with. Cost me seven years of my life. But I done got smarter. The next one's gonna be self-defense. The next one ain't gonna cost me nothing.

NOTES FOR THIS SPEECH:

If you need to make it shorter, you could drop the first and/or second paragraphs: **See Note 2.**

The language is appropriate for the period, but if it is not right for your purposes, be willing to change it: **See Note 3.**

An Afro-American accent is needed to match the lines; it is not important that your skin colour does: **See Note 7.**

36

THE PAVILION

Craig Wright

FIRST PERFORMANCES	Pittsburgh 2000; New York 2005
AWARDS	Nominated for the *Drama Desk Award for Outstanding Play*.
CHARACTER	Peter
PLAYED BY	J. Christopher O'Connor; Brian D'Arcy James
CHARACTER'S AGE	37
CHARACTER'S TYPE	He is a psychologist.
TIME AND PLACE	The present; The Pavilion, an old dance hall in the fictional town of Pine City, Minnesota.
SITUATION	Peter is telling Smoke, an old school friend now a minister, of the regrets in his life, in particular about his high school sweetheart Kari.

Peter: It's like when I said no to Kari back then, when I left town?
Smoke: Yeah?
Peter: It's like I got on the wrong train, you know? And I've been on this train now for twenty years, and Jesus, I don't want to go where this train is going, I really don't.
Smoke: Where do you want to go?
Peter: I want to go . . . I want to go where I maybe could have gone with her, you know? . . . if I had been more . . . I don't know, strong or something. When I saw Kari for the first time, Smoke, I'll never forget it; it was like the first or second week of high school and I walked into the audiovisual lab and there she was. And I swear – I couldn't have put this into words back then, but it's all I think about

lately – it was really like I recognized her or something. And I don't mean it like we'd met before or anything. We'd never met. It was just . . . it was as if in her face . . . in her beauty . . . I was finally seeing the beauty of everything, you know? . . . the unreachable beauty of the whole world that I'd always felt inside and tried to hold onto but never could, it was all in her. The whole universe had articulated itself in her. To me. That's just how I saw it. And I just knew that if I could be with her . . . by her side, you know? . . . then I could be alive and be a part of things. I'd at least have a chance. Now I know it sounds crazy, Smoke, I know, given everything that's happened, and there's a lot of water gone under the bridge, and a lot of time has passed, and there's been a lot of stupid shit and I've done most of it, but when I see her now, I still feel the same way. I look at her and I still see it, I see her face and I think, 'Oh, there you are . . . the world. Where have you been?' I love her, you know? I screwed up back then, there's no getting around it, but I love her. I think she's great. I love her.

NOTES FOR THIS SPEECH:

The character you are talking to, Smoke, has a few inconsequential lines: **See Note 1.**

You may feel like changing a word or two: **See Note 3.**

It would be a nice idea if you acted out first meeting Kari, including the change in your expression when you 'see' her: **See Note 5.**

This also applies to the latter part of the speech, when you can go from one emotion to the other, with big gear changes: **See Note 4.**

40s

37

INTIMATE EXCHANGES

Alan Ayckbourn

FIRST PERFORMANCES	Scarborough 1982; London 1984; Boston 1997
AWARDS	Nominated for the *Laurence Olivier Award for Best Comedy of the Year*.
	Lavinia Bertram [UK: Celia] nominated for the *Laurence Olivier Award for Best Comedy Performance of the year*.
CHARACTER	Toby
PLAYED BY	Robin Herford [UK]; Jack Gilpin [US]
CHARACTER'S AGE	early 40s
CHARACTER'S TYPE	He is a crumpled, red-faced man.
TIME AND PLACE	Today; England.
SITUATION	He is explaining to his wife Celia why their marriage is breaking up, why he drinks.

Toby: Look, I don't want to hurt your feelings again unnecessarily, Celia, but there are a whole load of more important reasons than you and your mother, why a man should turn to drink, I can tell you.

Celia: Yes, all right. You tell me, what are they?

Toby: O.K. You want a few? You want just a few of them? Here we go. Number one: I think the whole of life has become one long losing battle, all right? That's the first reason I'm drinking. Number two: I find myself hemmed in by an increasing number of quite appalling people all flying under the flags of various breeds of socialism, all of whom so far as I can gather are hell bent on courses of self-reward and self-remuneration that make the biggest capitalist look like Trotsky's Aunt Mildred. Number three: On the other hand, we have the rest of the country who don't even have the decency to pretend that they're doing it for the benefit of their fellow men. Ha ha. They're just grabbing hand over fist the most they can get for the minimum of effort by whatever grubby underhand means they can muster. Number four: We have half the men going around looking like women and half the women looking like men and the rest of us in the middle no longer knowing what the bloody hell we are. Number five: And the few remaining women who don't look like men are busy ripping their clothes off and prancing around on video cassettes and soft porn discs trying to persuade us that sex can be fun. Fun for God's sake, So can World War Three. Number six: – are you still with me? – We now have a police force that according to my paper anyway, is more dishonest than the people we're paying them to arrest. Don't, for God's sake, ask them the time, just hang on to your watch. Number seven: They've started this filthy floodlit cricket with cricketers wearing tin hats and advertisements for contraceptives on their boots. Number eight: You can no longer walk through the centre of any town anywhere in this country without being set upon by thousands of bald tattooed Neanderthals. Number nine: You can't get a hotel room in London for love nor money because they're all booked up by hordes of bloody foreigners in black berets busy wiring up suitcases full of bloody explosives to blow the rest of us up. And Number ten: whisky very, very shortly is going to be ten quid a bottle. Have I made my point, Celia?

Celia: I don't know what to say when you get like this. I just don't know.

Toby: I'd suggest they brought back hanging only they'd be sure to hang all the wrong people.

NOTES FOR THIS SPEECH:

'Trotsky': one of the leaders of communist Russia, later exiled by Stalin;

'cricket': national game of England; had always been played during the day, but is now also played under floodlights at night, to the dismay of traditionalists.

Celia's contributions are easy to re-act to, or to say yourself: **See Note 1**.

If you bring this up-to-date, you'll need to adjust the price of a bottle of whisky (£15 as of 2007): **See Note 3**.

If you equip yourself with a glass, and even a bottle, you can drink (and get more drunk) as the speech goes on: **See Notes 4 and 9**.

38

KVETCH

Steven Berkoff

FIRST PERFORMANCES	Los Angeles 1986; New York 1987; London 1991
AWARDS	Won the *Evening Standard Theatre Award for Best Comedy*.
CHARACTER	Hal
PLAYED BY	Mitch Kreindel [US]; Henry Goodman [UK]
CHARACTER'S AGE	40s
CHARACTER'S TYPE	He is the neighbour, who secretly would like a relationship with the host.
TIME AND PLACE	America now; middle-class home.
SITUATION	The characters speak their innermost thoughts and feelings out loud. Hal has been invited to dinner with his new friends, and is speaking his thoughts.

Hal: This is really a nice family . . . warm-hearted . . . kind . . . How nice of him to ask me . . . See, I'm warming up . . . I feel OK again . . . Maybe one day I'll have them over to me . . . Yeah, I'll make dinner for them . . . but I'm not a good cook . . . Oh, no, I've got the demons coming on . . . go 'way, go 'way!! I was happy before . . . Go away! . . . I can't be invited here again and not reciprocate . . . They maybe don't expect it but how many times can I be invited before reciprocating? Once . . . twice . . . three times? . . . I could make something simple and we'll have a few drinks . . . We'll eat in the kitchen and then go in the living room for coffee . . . Must I think of it now? . . . I'll make some snacks . . . just a little soupçon of everything . . . I'll get it from the deli and then we'll have it in the living room . . . Should we start in the living room with drinks then go to the kitchen? . . . But if I'm preparing something hot, say a soup, I'll have to leave them in the living room with a drink and run in and out . . . or . . . why not start off in the kitchen with drinks? . . . But then the stereo is in the living room . . . Oh, shit . . . we can play some music and have a few drinks and then go in the kitchen . . . or still better . . . I'll leave them with a drink and bring the stuff into the living room . . . But why shlepp it in the living room when the kitchen is supposed to be where you dine? . . . Unless I bring the stereo into the kitchen . . . but what if we go after to the living room for coffee? . . . I can't shlepp it back again . . . Maybe I'll buy another cassette deck . . . No, I'll put all the stuff in the living room and run in and out and most of the stuff will be cold anyway, except for the soup and the coffee . . . Mind you, it's cosy in the kitchen . . . There's a big wooden table in there . . . In the living room there's small tables so I'll have to take the salad round . . . to where people are sitting at the small tables . . . There's no centre table so we couldn't all face each other with a bottle in the middle . . . I'll have to walk around with the bottle . . . but at least there'll be space . . . but it won't be so warm as the kitchen . . . Oh, fuck it, we'll eat in there . . . that's fine . . . take the consequences . . . But it would be nice for them to see the living room . . . after, with coffee . . . not before . . . no after . . . not before? Wait! . . . We could eat in the living room if I brought the table into the centre, then I could put the bottle in the middle . . . That means taking the table from the kitchen . . . but then after we've eaten we'll have to sit in the living room with all the dirty dishes or make a fuss clearing them up whereas in the kitchen you just leave it all and say, let's stretch our feet in the living room . . . No, I know what to do . . . I'll kill myself instead . . . then I won't have to do anything . . . take an overdose or get run down by a truck . . . This is why God breathed life into me . . . to decide whether the table goes in the living room or in the kitchen . . . oooohh!

NOTES FOR THIS SPEECH:

You can always perform a cut-down version if it suits your purposes: **See Note 2.**

The language may need to be changed a little: **See Note 3.**

Your panic builds throughout the speech to ridiculous thoughts of suicide: **See Note 4.**

You are talking to the audience: **See Note 6.**

You can place the others downstage of you, and mime having the meal as you talk: **See Notes 8 and 9.**

39

PAUL

Howard Brenton

FIRST PERFORMANCES	London 2005
AWARDS	Nominated for the *Laurence Olivier Award for Best New Play*.
CHARACTER	Nero
PLAYED BY	Richard Dillane
CHARACTER'S AGE	late 40s
TYPE	Emperor of Rome, magnificently dressed.
TIME AND PLACE	AD 65; Roman prison.
SITUATION	The Emperor is making a clandestine visit to Paul, the Christian evangelist, who is in the death cell with other prisoners.

Nero: Oh please! I'm talking to the most intelligent dead man I've got hold of for years . . . don't spoil it with mumbo-jumbo. Listen. A state secret for the dead to take to their graves. In the next few years, Rome will destroy Judea.

Paul: Destroy?

Nero: We will flatten your country, Jew. Disarm and execute all the militias. All the fanatics on the roads, in the deserts. But not just the lunatics on the fringe. We will destroy all the priests, your Pharisees, your Sadducees, your Maccabeans. Then we will tear down the Jerusalem Temple, we won't leave a stone upon a stone. It will be so beautiful, like a song.

Paul: Destroy the Temple . . .

Nero: Destroy the whole country. It will no longer exist.

Paul: This is a . . . prophecy?

Nero: No, it's a well-advanced military plan. You won't be able to shout out about it tomorrow, you know, you'll have your tongues cut out.

Paul: Christ will come any day now . . .

Nero: He won't. And you know it. But look: when Judea is destroyed, your cult will have its chance. It can cut itself off from its Jewish roots, leave all that garbage about the Law of Moses behind. And basically your teaching is fine: it's quietist, it's authoritarian, its views on divorce are socially stabilising, it stresses respectful behaviour, particularly amongst women. And when you have priests, Antioch, Corinth, Byzantium, Ephesus and Rome, above all Rome . . . a good hierarchy of bribable gentlemen in fine robes, like any other religion . . . Why, then you will do business with the state. A hundred, two hundred years from now, Christianity could be the Empire's official religion.

Paul: Then why not release us now?

Nero: No no no, have you understood nothing? History needs your story. First the martyrdoms, the diaspora, the despair, then the full flowering of myth and poetry.

[Smiles.] You only preach two things, Paul: resurrection and the end of the world. Hardly any story at all! Christianity will need much more than that. But history will embellish: you as saints, me as one of the worst singers who ever lived. History is all lies. Goodnight gentlemen. *[Exits.]*

NOTES FOR THIS SPEECH:

'Pharisees, Sadducees, Maccabeans': different Jewish sects at that time.

You will need to act the other speeches, either by putting them into your lines, or by saying them yourself: See Note 1.

You are given a wonderfully funny last paragraph to be effective with, and to make an impressive exit.

Make sure you establish both Paul and the other prisoners at the start: See Note 8.

From PAUL by Howard Brenton, copyright © 2005 by Howard Brenton. Reprinted by permission of the publisher: www.nickhernbooks.co.uk. Amateur performing rights: info@nickhernbooks.demon.co.uk.

40

DEATH AND THE MAIDEN

Ariel Dorfman

FIRST PERFORMANCES	London 1991; New York 1992
AWARDS	**Won** the *Laurence Olivier Award for Best New Play.*
CHARACTER	Roberto
PLAYED BY	Bill Paterson [UK]; Gene Hackman [US]
CHARACTER'S AGE	40s
CHARACTER'S TYPE	He was a military torturer, now working as a doctor.
TIME AND PLACE	Now; in a country that has just emerged from totalitarian dictatorship. The home of a former torture victim and her husband.
SITUATION	Thinking she has recognised her former torturer, Paulina has tied up a visitor to their house – and he now confesses that he was in that line of business.

Roberto: I would put on the music because it helped me in my role, the role of good guy as they call it, I would put on Schubert because it was a way of gaining the prisoner's trust. But I also knew it was a way of alleviating their suffering. You've got to believe it was a way of alleviating the prisoners' suffering. Not only the music, but everything else I did. That's how they approached me, at first. The prisoners were dying on them, they told me, they needed someone to help care for them, someone they could trust. I've got a brother, who was a member of the secret services. You can pay the communists back for what they did to Dad, he told me one night – my father had a heart attack the day the peasants took over his land at Las Toltecas. The stroke paralysed him – he lost his capacity for speech, would spend hours simply looking at me; his eyes said, 'Do something'. But that's not why I accepted. The real real truth, it was for humanitarian reasons. We're at war, I thought, they want to kill me and my family, they want to install a totalitarian dictatorship, but even so, they still have the right to some form of medical attention. It was slowly, almost without realising how, that I became involved in more delicate operations, they let me sit in on sessions where my role was to determine if the prisoners could take that much torture, that much electric current. At first I told myself that it was a way of saving people's lives, and I did, because many times I told them – without it being true, simply to help the person who was being tortured – I ordered them to stop or the prisoner would die. But afterwards I began to – bit by bit, the virtue I was feeling turned into excitement – the mask of virtue fell off it and it, the excitement, it hid, it hid, it hid from me what I was doing, the swamp of what – . By the time Paulina Salas was brought in it was already too late. Too late . . . too late. A kind of – brutalisation took over my life, I began to really truly like what I was doing. It became a game. My curiosity was partly morbid, partly scientific. How much can this woman take? More than the other one? Does her sex dry up when you put the current through her? Can she have an orgasm under these circumstances? She is entirely in your power, you can carry out all your fantasies, you can do what you want with her.

Everything they have forbidden you since ever, whatever your mother ever urgently whispered you were never to do. Come on, Doctor, they would say to me, you're not going to refuse free meat, are you, one of them would sort of taunt me. His name was – let's see – they called him Bud, no, it was Stud – a nickname, because I never found out his real name. They like it, Doctor, Stud would say to me – all these bitches like it and if you put on that sweet little music of yours, they'll get even cosier. He would say this in front of the women, in front of Paulina Salas he would say it, and finally I, finally I – but not one ever died on me, not one of the women, not one of the men.

To the best of my memory, I took part in the – interrogation of 94 prisoners, including Paulina Salas. It is all I can say. I ask forgiveness.

NOTES FOR THIS SPEECH:

In the original production, this speech was played as a recorded cassette, with the others listening to it. There are many occasions when you repeat a word, almost as if you are searching for the phrase – a very natural 'real life' way of talking.

This is a bit long, and you can trim it by starting late into the speech at 'It was slowly,': See Note 2.

The very last bit could be done very simply, as a contrast to your earlier build: **See Note 5**.

You could do this speech either to another, or to the audience, as if speaking a confession: **See Note 6**.

41

CONVERSATIONS WITH MY FATHER

Herb Gardner

FIRST PERFORMANCES	Seattle 1990; New York 1994; London 1995
AWARDS	Judd Hirsch **won** the *Tony Award for Best Actor in a Play*.
CHARACTER	Eddie
PLAYED BY	Judd Hirsch [US and UK]
CHARACTER'S AGE	early 40s
CHARACTER'S TYPE	He is a bartender, and moves like an ex-boxer.
TIME AND PLACE	Late 1930s; a bar on Canal Street, New York.
SITUATION	Eddie, a Russian immigrant, owns a bar on Canal Street. He has changed his surname from Goldberg to Ross, and here he is giving fatherly advice to his infant son.

Eddie: *[Slaps the bar with his towel.]* O.K., Charlie, I know what's up, I know what you're doin' . . . *[Turns to stroller, smiling.]* And I *like* it! *[Approaching stroller with diaper and towel.]* You're *my kid* and you're not gonna say what you gotta say till you're damn good and ready. So I say *this* to you – don't let nobody push you around, and I include *myself* in that remark; got it? Because I would be tickled pink if the first Goddamn sentence you ever said was: 'Charlie Goldberg don't take shit from *nobody!' [Taking dirty diaper out of stroller.]* O.K., now I see you got a hold of your dick there. This don't bother me, be my guest. There's many schools of thought on grabbing your dick, pro and con. Me, I'm pro. I say, go to it, it's *your dick.* What you hope for is that someday some kind person out there will be as interested in it as you are. What you got a hold of there is optimism itself, what you got there in your hand is blind hope, which is the best kind. *[Grips edge of stroller.]* Everybody says to me, 'Hey, four bars into the toilet, *enough, forget* it, Eddie – a steady job tendin' bar, Eddie, maybe managin' a class place' – I say, 'I don't work for *no*body, baby, this ain't no employee's personality; I sweat, but I sweat for my *own*.' *[Deposits slug in Jukebox, making selection.]* And I ain't talking about no gin-mill, kid, I ain't talkin' about saloons and stand-up bars – I'm talkin' about what we got *here*, Charlie . . . I'm talkin' about America . . . *[From the Jukebox we begin to hear a full Chorus and Orchestra doing a gorgeous rendition of 'America, The Beautiful,' all strings and harps and lovely echoing voices.]* We give 'em *America*, Charlie – *[Takes in the place with a sweep of his hand as the MUSIC fills the room.]* We give 'em a Moose, we give 'em George Washington, we give 'em the red-white-and-blue, and mostly we give 'em, bar none, the greatest American invention of the last ten years – *Cocktails! [He flips a switch, illuminating the entire bar area, the mirror glows, a long strip of bulbs running the length of the shelf at the base of the mirror lights up the row of several dozen exotically colored cocktail-mix bottles; he points at the stroller.]* O.K., Canal Street, y'say – that's not a cocktail clientele out there, these are people who would suck after- shave lotion out of a wet wash-cloth – *[Advancing on stroller as Music builds.]* Nossir*! The trick here, all ya gotta remember, is nobody's equal but everybody *wants* to be – downtown slobs lookin' for uptown class, Goddamn Greenhorns lookin' to turn Yankee – New York style American Cocktails, Charlie! We liquor up these low-life nickel-dimers just long enough to bankroll an Uptown Lounge –

[MUSIC: He sings] 'Thine alabaster cities gleam,
Undimmed by human tears . . .'

Yessir, that's where we're *goin*' you and me; I'm lookin' *Up*town, kid, Madison, Lex – I got a *plan*, see, I'm *thinkin*' – *[Rising with the lush soprano.]* because there's only two ways a Jew *gets* Uptown; wanna get outa here, kid, you gotta *punch* your way out or *think* your way out. You're Jewish you gotta be smarter than everybody else; or cuter or faster or funnier. Or tougher. Because, basically, they want to kill you; this is true maybe thirty, thirty-five hundred years now and is not likely to change next Tuesday. It's not they don't want you in Moscow, or Kiev, or Lodz, or Jersey City: it's the earth, they don't want you on the *earth* is the problem; so the trick is to become necessary. If they need you they don' t kill you. Naturally, they're gonna hate you for needing you, but that beats they don't need

you and they kill you. Got it? *[His arms spread wide in conclusion.]* This, kid . . .
is the whole story.

NOTES FOR THIS SPEECH:

We have printed all the original stage instructions, including references to music. You
can just act listening to the music, or hum and sing the first few words, so the audience
know what it is that you are listening to: **See Note 1**.

Some of the words may need changing to suit your circumstances: **See Note 3**.

If this is too long for your purposes, you could cut the last paragraph. If you do, make
sure you build to a climax on 'Uptown Lounge': **See Notes 2 and 4**.

You would, of course put the invisible pram downstage of you, but be careful not
to tilt your face down so much that the audience cannot see your expressions: **See
Note 8**.

42

LIPS TOGETHER, TEETH APART

Terrence McNally

FIRST PERFORMANCES	New York 1991; Derby 1997
AWARDS	Nominated for the *Drama Desk Award for Outstanding New Play*.
CHARACTER	Sam
PLAYED BY	Nathan Lane [US]; John Guerrasio [UK]
CHARACTER'S AGE	40s
CHARACTER'S TYPE	He is a self-made business man.
TIME AND PLACE	Now; the wooden deck of a summer beach house in Long Island.
SITUATION	In a monologue not heard by the other characters, including his wife Sally, Sam talks of his mental turmoil.

Sam: My brain has become a collision course of random thoughts. Some trivial, but some well worth the wonder. Sometimes I think I'm losing my mind, I'm not sure of anything anymore. It's the same anxiety I have when I think I've forgotten how to tie my tie or tie my shoe laces or I've forgotten how to swallow my food and I'm going to choke on it. Three days ago I was standing in front of our bathroom mirror in terror because I couldn't knot my tie. I wanted to say 'Sally, please come in here and help me.' But I couldn't. What would she have thought? Last night I spit a piece of steak into my napkin, rather than risk swallowing it because I was afraid I would choke. Maybe it's trivial and that's why no one wants to talk about it, so I'm talking to myself. No one wants to listen to who we really are. Know somebody really. Know you leave shit stains in your underwear and pick your nose. Tell a woman you've forgotten how to swallow your food and she's in her car and out of your life before you can say 'Wait, there's more. Sometimes I have to think about someone else when I'm with you because I'm afraid I won't stay hard if I don't. Or how much I want to fuck the teenage daughter of the couple that lives three doors down. How my father takes all the air out of the room and I can't breathe when I'm with him. How if I could tear my breast open and rip out my heart and feed it to these seagulls in little raw pieces, that pain would be nothing to the one I already feel, the pain of your betrayal! How most afraid I am of losing you.' How can I tell you these things and there be love?

NOTES FOR THIS SPEECH:

Change the words if they do not add to the mood you want for this piece: **See Note 3**.

Your fear will build as the speech progresses: **See Note 4**.

The fact of her betrayal should come as a surprise: **See Note 5**.

You are talking to the audience: **See Note 6**.

43

THE LISBON TRAVIATA

Terrence McNally

FIRST PERFORMANCES	New York 1989; London 2003
AWARDS	Nominated for the *Drama Desk Award for Outstanding New Play*.
	Nathan Lane **won** the *Drama Desk Award for Outstanding Actor in a Play*.
CHARACTER	Mendy
PLAYED BY	Nathan Lane [US]; David Bamber [UK]
CHARACTER'S AGE	mid-aged
CHARACTER'S TYPE	He is out of shape, and takes some getting used to; he is a ferociously dedicated opera fan.
TIME AND PLACE	Now in America; Mendy's fussy bachelor apartment, New York.
SITUATION	Mendy is talking on the phone to his friend Paul about a legendary pirated recording of Maria Callas singing *La Traviata*, recorded in Lisbon. Stephen, an equally dedicated opera fan, is in the room.

Mendy: No, horses and camels are *Aida*. I wish you could remember the singers as well as you do the animals. *Traviata* begins at a party. Everyone is drinking champagne and being very gay. I'll ignore that! And then the tenor's father, the baritone, comes in and ruins everything, as fathers will. And then there's a gambling scene and in the last act she reads a letter, *Teneste la promessa*, and dies. You remember that much? Then you definitely remember *Traviata*. Now try to describe the soprano who was singing Violetta. Violetta is the heroine.

You're making me feel like Milton Cross. Skip it. Just tell me about the soprano. Other than the fact that you didn't like her, what can you tell me about her? 'Lousy' is a strong word, Paul. So is 'stunk.' I don't care about your opinion as a matter of fact! It's her name I'm after. I think you heard Maria Callas. That's a good question. I loved her so much. I still do. Everything about her. Anything. I'll take crumbs when it comes to Maria. Her time was so brief. That's why I was hoping maybe you could tell me something about her I didn't know. She's given me so much: pleasure, ecstasy, a certain solace, I suppose; memories that don't stop. This doesn't seem to be such a terrible existence with people like her to illuminate it. We'll never see her like again. How do you describe a miracle to someone who wasn't there? Do yourself a favor. Put on one of her records. *Puritani* or *Sonnambula* or *Norma*. If what you hear doesn't get to you, really speak to you, touch your heart, Paul, the truth of it, the intensity of the feeling . . . well, I can't imagine such a thing. I don't think we could be friends. I know we couldn't. There's a reason we called her La Divina but if you don't even remember who sang *Traviata* that night, there's no point in going on with this even if you did hear Callas. For people like you, it might as well have been Zinka Milanov. Skip that one too. Listen, thank you for your trouble. Enjoy the movie. No, I don't care what your grandfather thought of her either. The two of you heard the greatest singer who ever lived and you don't even remember it. Yes, she's dead, thanks to people like you! Murderer! I hope you hate the movie. *[He hangs up.]* God, I loathe the Portuguese.

NOTES FOR THIS SPEECH:

'Milton Cross': radio announcer who introduced the Metropolitan Opera radio broadcasts for many years;

'Zinka Milanov': famous soprano, and rival to Maria Callas.

Although you are 'mid-aged', Nathan Lane was in his 30s when he played the role.

You start off pleasantly, and build to a murderous rage: See Note 4.

You can have a lot of fun 'listening' to the other side of the telephone conversation; a real handset could help too: See Note 9.

44

DUMB SHOW

Joe Penhall

FIRST PERFORMANCES	London 2005; Costa Mesa 2005
AWARDS	Douglas Hodge nominated for the *Evening Standard Theatre Award for Best Actor*.
CHARACTER	Barry
PLAYED BY	Douglas Hodge [UK]; Michael McShane [US]
CHARACTER'S AGE	40s
CHARACTER'S TYPE	He is a top television star.
TIME AND PLACE	Now; five-star London hotel room.
SITUATION	Barry is talking to some agents, after becoming the target of tabloid newspaper investigations of his wife's death.

Barry: She went back into hospital just after you . . . it was everywhere, you know . . . nothing they could do . . . *[Gestures.]* She went home for a while and they put her on a, you know they gave her oxygen in a tank which helped for a bit but she had so little . . . *[Gestures. Stares.]* She didn't want to go into a hospice, you see . . . she wanted to be at home with . . . with her . . . ponies. I'd go round there a bit just to keep her company . . . comfort her when she . . . she sometimes would . . . cry in the night and so on . . . she couldn't sleep . . . she'd just be thinking about . . . I'd hear her crying to herself quietly and . . . uh, broke my heart really . . . She was just . . . very frightened, you see . . . poor old thing . . . *[Pause.]* I'd try and be there to hold her hand. Give her a cuddle and cheer her up a bit . . . I took her out a bit when she wanted to get some air. I took her around a few of the old . . . all her favourite places . . . took her for a curry, to her favourite curry place down in the village, she wanted to say hi, or bye . . . but you know there was no tables, you see, we couldn't get a table and nobody was, nobody she knew was on that night and so it was a bit of a . . . it was just a . . . uh . . . I felt so sorry for. She was just being friendly. She just wanted to say goodbye. *[Pause.]* I took her to the market . . . took her around all the old stalls, the cheese stall, the flower stall, the fishmonger, you know the kind of . . . so she could tell them. Tell them she was actually going to die and all that. They didn't believe her. I told them, I said . . . *[Gestures.]* They didn't believe me. Thought I was joking. Typical. *[Pause.]* So you see it was all very . . . six weeks it took. Seventeen years of marriage all gone in . . . *[Pause.]* It was . . . very, very sad really . . . very sad.

NOTES FOR THIS SPEECH:

You have lots of unfinished thoughts and gear changes; be careful you find all the varieties, and do not play it all as gloomy: **See Note 4**.

As a television star, you will be excellent at presentation; this could then change surprisingly into real emotions: **See Note 5**.

45

LOST IN YONKERS

Neil Simon

FIRST PERFORMANCES	Washington 1991; New York 1991; London 1992
AWARDS	Won *The Pulitzer Prize for Drama*, and the *Tony Award for Best Play*, and the *Drama Desk Award for Outstanding New Play*; nominated for the *Laurence Olivier Award for Best Comedy*.
CHARACTER	Eddie
PLAYED BY	Mark Blum [US]; Rolf Saxon [UK]
CHARACTER'S AGE	41
CHARACTER'S TYPE	He is a father beset with financial worries.
TIME AND PLACE	1942; an apartment in Yonkers, New York.
SITUATION	Crushed by debt, Eddie is explaining to his two children Jay and Arty that they are to move in here with their Grandmother for the duration.

Eddie: We're not rich people, boys. I know that doesn't come as a surprise to you . . . but I'm going to tell you something now I hoped I'd never have to tell you in my life . . . The doctors, the hospital, cost me everything I had . . . I was broke and I went into debt . . . So I went to a man . . . A loan shark . . . A moneylender . . . I couldn't go to a bank because they don't let you put up heartbreak and pain as collateral . . . A loan shark doesn't need collateral . . . His collateral is your desperation . . . So he gives you his money . . . And he's got a clock . . . And what it keeps time of is your promise . . . If you keep your promise, he turns off the clock . . . and if not, it keeps ticking . . . and after a while, your heart starts ticking louder than his clock . . . Understand something. This man kept your mother alive . . . It was his painkillers that made her last days bearable . . . And for that I'm grateful . . . Jay! Remember what I taught you about taking things from people?

Jay: Never take because you'll always be obligated.

Eddie: So you never take for yourself . . . But for someone you love, there comes a time when you have no choice . . . There's a man in New York I owe . . . Nine thousand dollars . . . I could work and save four more years and I won't have nine thousand dollars . . . He wants his money this year. To his credit, I'll say one thing. He sent flowers to the funeral. No extra charge on my bill . . .

Jay: Pop –

Eddie: Let me finish . . . There is no way I can pay this man back . . . So what'll he do? Kill me? . . . Maybe . . . If he kills me, he not only loses his money, it'll probably cost him again for the flowers for *my* funeral . . . I needed a miracle . . . And the miracle happened . . . This country went to war . . . A war between us and the Japanese and the Germans . . . And if my mother didn't come to this country thirty-five years ago, I could have been fighting for the other side . . . Except I don't think they're putting guns in the hands of Jews over there . . . Let me tell you something. I love this country. Because they took in the Jews. They took in the Irish, the Italians and everyone else . . . Remember this. There's a lot of Germans in this country fighting for America, but there are no Americans over there fighting for Germany . . . I hate this war, and God forgive me for saying this, but it's going to save my life . . . There are jobs I can get now that I could never get before . . . And I got a job . . . I'm working for a company that sells scrap iron . . . I thought you threw scrap iron away. Now they're building ships with it . . . Without even the slightest idea of what I'm doing, I can make that nine thousand dollars in less than a year . . .

Jay: That's great, Pop.

Eddie: Don't say it till I finish . . . The factories that I would sell to are in the South . . . Georgia, Kentucky, Louisiana, Texas, even New Mexico . . . I'd be gone about ten months . . . Living in trains, buses, hotels, any place I can find a room . . . We'd be free and clear and back together again in less than a year . . . Okay? . . . So now comes the question, where do you two live while I'm gone?

NOTES FOR THIS SPEECH:

'collateral': security pledged for the payment of a loan.

You will need to act out the lines by your children: **See Note 1**.

Make sure you are as varied as possible as you talk of your wife's death, of your hatred of loan sharks and of the war, and of the possibility of success: **See Notes 4 and 5**.

46

TWILIGHT: LOS ANGELES, 1992

Anna Deavere Smith

FIRST PERFORMANCES	Los Angeles 1993; New York 1994
AWARDS	Nominated for the *Tony Award for Best Play*.
	Anna Deavere Smith nominated for the *Tony Award for Best Actress in a Play*.
CHARACTER	Owen
PLAYED BY	Anna Deavere Smith
CHARACTER'S AGE	40s
CHARACTER'S TYPE	The author performed all the different characters in this play as a one-woman show. This character is a former range manager of the Beverly Hills Gun Club.
TIME AND PLACE	1992; Los Angeles.
SITUATION	He is recounting what happened to his business after the riots.

Owen: After the riots our business went up forty percent, maybe as much as
fifty percent.
We have a membership here that shoots,
riots or no riots,
but because of the feeling of
danger overall in the community . . .
Long time ago you used to say there's some areas of LA County
where you couldn't walk
after dark,
and it's progressed to the point where you say, 'Gee,

there's no place
safe
in LA County, daylight *or* dark.'
People are looking for an opportunity to defend themselves.
They just need something,
and this is one of the places they come.
Shooting is a skill just like anything else.
A deadeye?
Is a very good shot.
Yes,
I am a deadeye.
I'm not a natural one.
I spent
couple years in Vietnam,
and that will make you good if nothing else.
You don't want to get over there and hit your foot.
Sure,
a lot of these are handguns.
If you look at the top row, those are the smaller-caliber guns,
twenty-twos,
and then as you work your way on down to the bottom row,
that's the forty-fives.
I guess you'd say the least powerful at the top
to the most powerful at the bottom.
Probably the most powerful here
are the forty-fives.
This is a forty-four
Magnum gun,
probably the most powerful handgun that we have here.
I usually start people with a thirty-eight.
One of the most popular for the drive-bys are the nine millimeters,
But the gang members and some of the more organised groups out
there are using everything,
everything.
There's no question about it, they
are probably better armed than we are.

If you speak this piece as it is written, and so take a tiny pause at the end of each line and nowhere else, it will give you a naturalistic delivery. The speech is laid out the way the author wrote it (and, yes, she did win an acting nomination for playing the many different roles in the play, including this male one); you can shorten it to meet your needs: **See Note 2**.

The more delight you have in describing the guns, the more downbeat you can be in realising that the gangs out-gun you: **See Note 5**.

You can place the imaginary rows of guns downstage of you, so we can see your delight in talking about them: **See Note 8**.

47

HOW I LEARNED TO DRIVE

Paula Vogel

FIRST PERFORMANCES	New York 1997; London 1998
AWARDS	Won *The Pulitzer Prize for Drama*; and the *Drama Desk Award for Outstanding New Play*.
	David Morse **won** the *Drama Desk Award for Outstanding Actor in a Play*.
CHARACTER	Peck
PLAYED BY	David Morse [US]; Kevin Whately [UK]
CHARACTER'S AGE	40s
CHARACTER'S TYPE	He is a hero type, like his name-sake Gregory Peck; but he is also a child abuser.
TIME AND PLACE	Today; America.
SITUATION	Peck is very gently manipulating his young female friend into getting into a compromising situation with him, as he teaches her how to fish for pompano.

Peck: Okay. You don't want to lean over the bridge like that – pompano feed in shallow water, and you don't want to get too close – they're frisky and shy little things – wait, check your line. Yep, something's been munching while we were talking.

Okay, look: We take the sand flea and you take the hook like this – right through his little sand flea rump. Sand fleas should always keep their backs to the wall. Okay. Cast it in, like I showed you. That's great! I can taste that pompano now, sautéed with some pecans and butter, a little bourbon – now – let it lie on the bottom – now, reel, jerk, reel, jerk –

Look – look at your line. There's something calling, all right. Okay, tip the rod up – not too sharp – hook it – all right, now easy, reel and then rest – let it play.

And reel – play it out, that's right – really good! I can't believe it! It's a pompano. – Good work! Way to go! You are an official fisherman now. Pompano are hard to catch. We are going to have a delicious little –

What? Well, I don't know how much pain a fish feels – you can't think of that. Oh, no, don't cry, come on now, it's just a fish – the other guys are going to see you. – No, no, you're just real sensitive, and I think that's wonderful at your age – look, do you want me to cut it free? You do?

Okay, hand me those pliers – look – I'm cutting the hook – okay? And we're just going to drop it in – no I'm not mad. It's just for fun, okay? There – it's going to swim back to its lady friend and tell her what a terrible day it had and she's going to stroke him with her fins until he feels better, and then they'll do something alone together that will make them both feel good and sleepy. . . .

[PECK bends down, very earnest.] I don't want you to feel ashamed about crying. I'm not going to tell anyone, okay? I can keep secrets. You know, men cry all the time. They just don't tell anybody, and they don't let anybody catch them. There's nothing you could do that would make me feel ashamed of you. Do you know that? Okay. *[PECK straightens up, smiles.]* Do you want to pack up and call it a day? I tell you what – I think I can still remember – there's a really neat tree house where I used to stay for days. I think it's still here – it was the last time I looked. But it's a secret place – you can't tell anybody we've gone there – least of all your mom or your sisters. – This is something special just between you and me. Sound good? We'll climb up there and have a beer and some crab salad – okay?

NOTES FOR THIS SPEECH:

'pompano': fish that looks like a fat mackerel.

You can always trim this speech if you find it a bit long: See Note 2.

The audience will enjoy seeing you change as you entice the young girl into your world: See Note 4.

There is a danger that if you talk down to the imaginary little girl, you will hide your eyes from the audience; kneeling down would help, as well as allowing us to see your 'accidental' touching of her: See Note 8.

It would probably be best to mime all the fishing tackle (so make sure you learn and do the correct moves): See Note 9.

48

IT'S RALPH

Hugh Whitemore

FIRST PERFORMANCES	London 1981
AWARDS	Nominated for the *Laurence Olivier Award for Best Comedy*.
CHARACTER	Ralph
PLAYED BY	Jack Shepherd
CHARACTER'S AGE	late 40s
CHARACTER'S TYPE	He is an old friend from the past.
TIME AND PLACE	Today; a crumbling English country cottage.
SITUATION	Ralph has arrived at the cottage, and is making himself more at home than his hosts Clare and Andrew would like.

Ralph: This'll make you laugh. True story. The first time I saw you on TV. When was it? – fifteen, twenty years ago. Money was short and I'd got myself a job as a shop assistant. Bond Street. Selling cameras. Every lunchtime I used to go to a little café, a little sandwich bar, near Hanover Square. When it was warm and sunny they'd put tables on the pavement, and there I'd sit and eat my lunch. One day I noticed a couple sitting at the next table. They were youngish, about my age, and they were very beautiful, very happy in each other's company. The following day they came back and sat at the same table. I watched them quite openly. I watched how they smiled at each other. How their hands touched. Her fingers on his arm. They knew I was watching them. They seemed to enjoy it. They came back the next day and the next, and on the fifth day, as they were leaving, the girl put a slip of paper on my table. On it was written the name of a hotel and a room number and a simple message: 'This afternoon at five.' I made some excuse and left work early. I went to the hotel and found the room. The girl opened the door. She smiled and said, 'Hi, I'm Joanne.' She was Australian. She took her clothes off and lay on the bed. 'Don't be shy,' she said. Then the bathroom door opened and the man came in. Robert. She called him Bobby. He was naked. Huge erection. I'd never had three-way sex before. It was amazing. Later, in the evening, as we lay there, the three of us together (somewhat knackered, as you can imagine), the girl, Joanne, reached forward and switched on the TV at the foot of the bed. The first thing I saw was your face, smiling at us. I couldn't believe it. Joanne was going to change channels, but I stopped her. 'I know that man,' I said, 'we were once great friends.' You were doing one of your political things: making fun of the Prime Minister — I forget which one it was.

I stayed the night with them. The following morning I asked Robert for their address in Australia. 'Let's keep in touch,' I said. 'No,' he said, 'we can't do that; we must never see each other again. Joanne is my sister.'

Good story, eh?

NOTES FOR THIS SPEECH:

'knackered': to be completely exhausted.

The more we think you are just a watcher of lovers, the more the paper invitation will be a surprise. And the ending should be equally surprising for us: **See Note 5**.

Make sure you put your listeners into good positions: **See Note 8**.

over 50s

49

THE MARRIAGE OF BETTE AND BOO

Christopher Durang

FIRST PERFORMANCES	New York 1985
AWARDS	Nominated for the *Drama Desk Award for Outstanding New Play*.
	Joan Allen [Bette] nominated for the *Drama Desk Award for Outstanding Actress in a Play*.
CHARACTER	Father Donnally
PLAYED BY	Richard B. Shull
CHARACTER'S AGE	50s
CHARACTER'S TYPE	He is a local Catholic priest, and could be any reasonable age (the original was in his 50s).
TIME AND PLACE	Now; in America; a Catholic retreat.
SITUATION	Father Donnally is leading a retreat on Christ and the Wedding Feast, and carefully avoids questions from the unmarried Emily.

Father Donnally: *[Laughs, nervously.]* Please don't talk when I'm talking. *[Starts his speech.]* Young marrieds have many problems to get used to. For some of them this is the first person of the opposite sex the other has ever known. The husband may not be used to having a woman in his bathroom. The wife may not be used to a strong masculine odor in her boudoir. Or then the wife may not cook well enough. How many marriages have floundered on the rocks of ill-cooked bacon? *[Pause.]* I used to amuse friends by imitating bacon in a saucepan. Would anyone like to see that? *[He looks around for approval. FATHER DONNALLY falls* *to the ground and does a fairly good – or if not good, at least unabashedly peculiar – imitation of bacon, making sizzling noises and contorting his body to represent becoming crisp. Toward the end, he makes sputtering noises into the air. Then he stands up again. All present applaud with varying degrees of approval or incredulity.]*

I also do coffee percolating. *[He does this.]* Pt. Pt. Ptptptptptptptptpt. Bacon's better. But things like coffee and bacon are important in a marriage, because they represent things that the wife does to make her husband happy. Or fat. *[Laughs.]* The wife cooks the bacon, and the husband brings home the bacon. This is how St. Paul saw marriage, although they probably didn't really eat pork back then, the curing process was not very well worked out in Christ's time, which is why so many of them followed the Jewish dietary laws even though they were Christians. I know I'm glad to be living now when we have cured pork and plumbing and showers rather than back when Christ lived. Many priests say they wish they had lived in Christ's time so they could have met Him; that would, of course, have been very nice, but I'm glad I live now and that I have a shower.

I'm not ready for questions yet, Emily. *[He sips his wine.]* Man and wife, as St. Paul saw it. Now the woman should obey her husband, but that's not considered a very modern thought, so I don't even want to talk about it. All right, don't obey your husbands, but if chaos follows, don't blame me. The Tower of Babel as an image of chaos has always fascinated me.

Bette: Put your hand down, Emily.

Father Donnally: *[To BETTE.]* Thank you. Now I don't mean to get off the point. The point is husband and wife, man and woman, Adam and rib. I don't want to dwell on the inequality of the sexes because these vary from couple to couple – sometimes the man is stupid, sometimes the woman is stupid, sometimes both are stupid. The point is man and wife are joined in holy matrimony to complete each other, to populate the earth and to glorify God. That's what it's for. That's what life is for. If you're not a priest or a nun, you normally get married.

Yes, I know, you're not married, Emily. Not everyone gets married. But my comments today are geared toward the *married* people here. Man and wife are helpmates. She helps him, he helps her. In sickness and in health. Anna Karenina should not have left her husband, nor should she have jumped in front of a train.

135

Imitating the sizzling bacon and the coffee pot gives you glorious opportunities for comedic business (and perhaps an indication that you are avoiding talking about more serious things.)

The interruption could be treated by you as another attempt by Emily to speak: **See Note 1**.

You often let your negative feelings about people show: **See Note 5**.

The last sentence begins as an extension of the wifely duties as defined by you, but the 'down to earth' awfulness of the train should be both shocking and funny. **See Note 5**.

50

STANLEY

Pam Gems

FIRST PERFORMANCES	London 1996; New York 1996
AWARDS	Won the *Evening Standard Theatre Award for Best Play*, and the *Laurence Olivier Award for Best New Play*; nominated for the *Tony Award for Best Play*.
	Anthony Sher won the *Laurence Olivier Award for Best Actor*; nominated for the *Tony Award for Best Actor in a Play*.
CHARACTER	Stanley
PLAYED BY	Anthony Sher [UK and US]
CHARACTER'S AGE	60s
CHARACTER'S TYPE	He is the famous English artist Stanley Spencer; he never lost his rough edges despite being taken up by the smart set.
TIME AND PLACE	1950s; England, Cookham Village, the promenade.
SITUATION	He is painting a canvas, and he talks to it as if it were Hilda, his first wife now dead. He always kept his paints in a pram.

Stanley: *[Sings.]* 'Improve thy knowledge with due care, In all thy life thyself prepare' . . .

Remember when I came down to Devon that time? After you'd been ill? And they wouldn't let me stay with you, so I slept in a beach hut, and you said the sea was like opals?

This is for your altar piece. I'm really trying to hang on to it – simplicity – not like something separate on a shelf but in me . . . real, alive. Then I can do you properly. Oh I wish I could smell you . . . that buttery smell of your hair . . . your body smelling of cobnuts. I keep the cupboard shut on your clothes so it won't go away, the smell. I pick up your shoes, I use your comb. I've even got your flannel.

Oh ducky. I feel so close to you. You're in me – you-and-me. The only being I can talk to, that I've ever wanted to talk to. It's so wonderful talking to you, and never having to be careful of what I say, or whether you won't understand – I feel you understand everything now. That you're looking out for me. It makes me feel closer to Heaven with you there. Specially after work, when I'm tired. I see this great picture of God and all His Angels sitting on these beautiful three-dimensional clouds and on His left hand sits Bach and on His right hand Stanley! I'm only joking of course.

You'll love this when it's done. I'm going to do Christ glorying in His gorgeousness, I want him in a great gallivanting, lying-down sprawl on the greensward. Rather far from Holy Writ I daresay, but I don't know why they think what I'm doing is pagan, what am I supposed to paint? I don't know the flowers around Galilee, the flowers I know are buttercups and daisies. It's no good doing palm trees – I'm English, so I do the Englishness of things. You do the things you love. For His glory.

You know what I think, Hilda? I think an artist is the mediator between God and man. He could even be next in divinity to the saint. Like the saint he performs miracles. With God's help of course. God's at his elbow, telling him what to rub out. *[Pause.]*

You didn't look after yourself, you know. You should have done, for me and the girls. You should have thought about yourself more, made sure you were happy. Then you wouldn't have been so ill and we wouldn't have to . . . *[He can't go on. He takes a moment to recover himself.]*

I'm not lonely. I loved being with you, but I enjoy it here on my own. You're here in my imagination. In some ways it's better. I make up your answers for you and sometimes they – well, sometimes they suit me better. I hope you don't mind. People often ask me if I'm lonely. I say no, I'm not lonely. I've had a great love, do you see? I've been blessed. God blessed me with a talent and a great love. Now I'm alone to get on with the work. Sorrow and sadness is not me. *[He gets up, straightens, looks down at the canvas.]*

Beautifully done. *[He packs up his things, puts them on the pram. And goes.]*

'greensward': grassy turf.

Because the part of Stanley needed to be played at different ages, Anthony Sher, then in his late 40s, was cast in the role.

The journey you would make in playing the entire part needs to be done in this one speech: **See Note 4**.

This really does need an English accent, and the first line could be sung as an English hymn: **See Note 7**.

Naturally the (invisible) canvas will be downstage of you, although it would be quite appropriate to use a real paint brush: **See Notes 8 and 9**.

51

WRONG MOUNTAIN

David Hirson

FIRST PERFORMANCES	New York 2000
AWARDS	Daniel Davis nominated for the *Tony Award for Best Featured Actor in a Play*.
CHARACTER	Maurice
PLAYED BY	Daniel David
CHARACTER'S AGE	over 50
CHARACTER'S TYPE	He is a soft-bellied, sagging-faced older man with a thatch of thinning hair dyed an improbable shade of red.
TIME AND PLACE	Now; America, the stage of a theatre.
SITUATION	The Artistic Director makes a 'curtain' speech before the first night of a new play at a Festival.

Maurice: Last year, a young writer cracked open our souls with a heroic tale of how one man's talent and dexterity emboldened half the population of an occupied Polish village to laugh defiantly in the face of the Holocaust. That play – *Fingerpuppets of Hope*, by Daniel Eisenberg . . . *[MAURICE, applauding too.]* . . . I agree . . . *[Continuing.]* . . . not only walked away with our top prize – the coveted Lila B. Hirschorn Memorial Scepter – but set a standard of excellence that seemed, at the time, unmatchable. Yet if we have learned anything from our first two authors, it is that the artistic imagination, which mysteriously takes flight like some . . . *[Improvising expansively and absurdly, his voice quivering with emotion.]* . . . cockamamie, madcap, semideranged whippoorwill . . . continually establishes a new standard of excellence, soaring to heights previously undreamed of! Our final offering is no exception. Fearlessly addressing many of the most vexing issues that touch our lives and rend our society today, a gifted poet and playwright captures the *Zeitgeist* in a work that is part hallucination, part meditation, part documentary, and part prayer. *[Pause.]* Ladies and gentlemen . . . *Wrong Mountain* . . . by Adolf Hitler.

NOTES FOR THIS SPEECH:

'cockamamie': ludicrous; nonsensical;

'whippoorwill': American bird that sings in the evening;

'Zeitgeist': spirit of the present time.

You are building to a totally unexpected ending: **See Notes 4 and 5**.

You are talking to your audience: **See Note 6**.

52

A MONTH OF SUNDAYS

Bob Larbey

FIRST PERFORMANCES	Southampton 1985; London 1986; New York 1987
AWARDS	Won the *Evening Standard Theatre Award for Best Comedy*.
CHARACTER	Cooper
PLAYED BY	George Cole [UK]; Jason Robards [US]
CHARACTER'S AGE	late 60s
CHARACTER'S TYPE	He is retired; rather frail but lively of mind.
TIME AND PLACE	Sunday; Cooper's room in the Home for the Elderly somewhere in the UK.
SITUATION	Cooper is waiting for his regular delivery of food for breakfast, and telling the audience how things are at the rest home.

Cooper: The Panzers will be coming soon. They're in the kitchen now, loading up for the first offensive of the day. Fuel on board – tea, coffee, orange juice. Ammunition on board – porridge, cereals, eggs, bacon, armour-piercing sausages. The crews stand ready, smart and starched. Then a signal from the Divisional Commander, Mrs. Simmons, and they rumble out into the corridors, cutting a swathe of clatter through the silence of an early morning. There's little resistance – the odd cry of, 'I don't want any breakfast.' Quite useless – the breakfast is left in any case. 'I don't want any breakfast' is translated as meaning, 'But nevertheless I do want to lie here looking at the breakfast I don't want to eat.' Some of course – the Zombies – aren't really sure which meal it is they're supposed to be eating. That's a victory of sorts, I suppose. At least it robs the

Panzers of the satisfaction of knowing that their dawn Blitzkrieg has been a total success. They can hardly triumph at someone eating his breakfast when that someone is quite convinced he's eating his lunch. My friend Aylott once devised an ingenious plan. He dropped his upper dentures into his scrambled eggs. The dentures were retrieved and of course the scrambled eggs were taken away and just for that morning, the Panzers forgot to bring him back a fresh plateful. We formed an Escape Committee last summer, Aylott and I. It entailed causing a huge explosion of porridge in the kitchen and Aylott and I making our way to Switzerland disguised as nuns. He was much better in the summer, Aylott. *[He hears a noise in the corridor.]*

Ah, the Panzers! *[There is a tap at the door.]*

[Loudly.] I should think twice, Fritz! I've got a twenty-five pounder trained on the door!

NOTES FOR THIS SPEECH:

'Panzers': mechanized tank divisions that spearheaded the German attacks in World War Two;

'Blitzkrieg': name for a sudden lightning attack, much used by the Germans in World War Two (strangely, based on idea developed by an English military man, but rejected by his superiors in the 1930s);

'Fritz': one of the names used by the British for German soldiers;

'twenty-five pounder': large cannon.

Use a very different tone when talking of the plan to escape: **See Note 4**.

Make sure you have a nice gear change between talking of your friend Aylott, and hearing a noise in the corridor – a good opportunity to show your reactions to (unheard) noises off: **See Note 5**.

You are talking to the audience: **See Note 6**.

Make sure you place the door downstage of you: **See Note 8**.

53

THE RETREAT FROM MOSCOW

William Nicholson

FIRST PERFORMANCES	Chichester 1999; New York 2003
AWARDS	Nominated for the *Tony Award for Best Play*.
	Ben Chaplin [US: Jamie] nominated for the *Tony Award for Best Performance by a Featured Actor in a Play*.
CHARACTER	Edward
PLAYED BY	Edward Hardwicke [UK]; John Lithgow [US]
CHARACTER'S AGE	late 50s
TYPE	A teacher at a boys' school, perfectly at home with his daily crossword.
TIME AND PLACE	Now; the family home in England.
SITUATION	The father is talking to his son Jamie as he dissects his marriage to Alice, and how it all went wrong.

Edward: You know how it's been with Alice. For, oh, a long time now. Years. There was an incident a few weeks ago, at school. Maybe she told you about it.
Jamie: No.
Edward: She found me in the staffroom. There was something I'd forgotten, or failed to do, something very minor. She went for me in front of my colleagues, which I consider unacceptable. What could I do? I walked out of the staffroom. To avoid the embarrassment of it. She came after me, saying, 'Talk to me. Answer me. Look at me.' I walked faster and faster, not really thinking where I was going. She followed. 'Talk to me. Answer me. Look at me.' I went out onto the playing

fields. She followed. 'Turn and face me, you coward. You can't run for ever.' And of course, the playing fields don't go on for ever. So I turned back, and there she was. I tried to walk past her, but she kept in my way, shouting at me. 'Talk to me. Answer me. Look at me.' Then she started to take off her clothes. She took off her jersey, and threw it at me. She was wearing a T-shirt underneath, like a teenager. She took that off, threw it at me. Then her skirt. Then her bra. It was unbearable. She looked pitiful, standing there, trembling, in the middle of the playing field. So of course I had to turn and face her. And she said 'There. I've made you look at me at last.'

Jamie: I didn't know it was that bad.

Edward: Sometimes I think she's mad. And then, at other times . . . It's not simple, somehow.

Jamie: She's not mad.

Edward: No, of course not. But you must admit she's not like most people.

NOTES FOR THIS SPEECH:

The other speeches will be easy to act: **See Note 1**.

This is quite a short speech, so the pauses when the wife is undressing might be effective (and time-filling).

Make sure that Alice is downstage of you when she undresses: **See Note 8**.

54

FORTUNE'S FOOL

Ivan Turgenev, adapted by Mike Poulton

FIRST PERFORMANCES	Chichester 1996; New York 2002
AWARDS	Nominated for the *Tony Award for Best Play*.
	Alan Bates **won** the *Tony Award for Best Actor in a Play*, **and** the *Drama Desk Award for Outstanding Actor in a Play*.
CHARACTER	Kuzovkin
PLAYED BY	Alan Bates [UK and US]
CHARACTER'S AGE	50s
CHARACTER'S TYPE	He is an impoverished Russian gentleman.
TIME AND PLACE	Mid-nineteenth century; a Russian country manor house.
SITUATION	Kuzovkin is telling Olga about how her mother dealt with her husband's infidelities, how her supposed father died, and that he is her real father.

Kuzovkin: I think . . . How would I truly judge? I know nothing except by feeling – but I think the truth is that her sanity began to fail. She would go into the icon room and stand crossing herself before the holy images. Smiling sometimes. And all the time my heart was aching for her sorrows. She could hardly eat. Nobody spoke to her except me. The servants moved about the house like ghosts. Can you imagine that? That strange unnatural silence. In the evening she would talk to me – in here, this room – and it was all about him . . . until one night, suddenly it was as if her love for him had broken. She turned to me, and looked at me, and after a long, long silence when I could feel my heart beating as though

it would explode in my breast – I loved her so hopelessly – and I knew . . . I knew
. . . what she was going to say, and oh . . . quite suddenly, and calmly she said:
'Vassily Semyonitch, I know how deeply and purely you love me, and I know at
last that he has never loved me, and that he will never feel anything for me but
contempt and loathing . . . But I feel for you . . . I need . . .' And she laid her head
on my breast . . . And, oh Olya! I didn't know what to say or do. We were both lost.
Forgive me, please forgive me. I can't tell you any more about it. It's not right that
I should.

Olga: How did he die?

Kuzovkin: The very next day . . . As soon as it began to grow light I went out into
the fields. I remember the skylarks. I was still in a dream. Somebody brought the
news – rode over from the next village. Your father had fallen from his horse.
They'd carried his body into a priest's house. I watched your mother go off in the
carriage. Dear Lord, we thought she would go mad. She was hardly alive herself
– right up until the time you were born. And then, as you know, she never
recovered – it was as if, for the rest of her life, she inhabited some other, better
world. *[He sinks.]*

Olga: And I . . . I am your daughter. Is there any proof of this?

Kuzovkin: *[Shaken.]* Merciful God! Proof? Olga Petrovna, I have proof of nothing
– there is no proof! That I would dare! Had I not made such a fool of myself
yesterday the truth would have gone with me to my grave. I'd sooner have died.
Why the good Lord did not strike me down in my folly I shall never know. Until
yesterday not a soul . . . I would not even whisper it to my own soul . . . Dear God!

NOTES FOR THIS SPEECH:

You will need to act the missing speeches, especially including the wish for proof that
she is your daughter: See Note 1.

Much of this speech needs to be quietly spoken – a theatrical challenge. It could make
a good screen test audition: See Note 7.

Make sure Olga is in the right place for you (and that you are speaking for so long
because you are not letting her get a word in.): See Note 8.

INDEX OF PLAYWRIGHTS

INDEX OF PLAYS

INDEX OF ACTORS

AWARD LIST FROM 1980 TO 2006

(* = winner)

In the US the nominations are taken from the *Tony Awards for Best Play*; and the *Drama Desk Awards for Outstanding Play/Outstanding New Play*, together with the winner of the *Pulitzer Prize for Drama*.

In the UK the nominations are taken from the *Evening Standard Theatre Awards for Best Play* and *Best Comedy*; and the *Laurence Olivier Awards for Best Play of the Year/Best New Play*, and *Best Comedy of the Year/Best Comedy/Best New Comedy*.

(In order to put the plays in their proper groupings, the year is for the period that the award covered, not necessarily the year in which the award was given.)

1980

The Pulitzer Prize for Drama:
Crimes of the Heart – Beth Henley

Tony Award nominations for Best Play:
A Lesson from Aloes – Athol Fugard
A Life – Hugh Leonard
*Amadeus – Peter Shaffer
Fifth of July – Lanford Wilson

Drama Desk Award nominations for Outstanding New Play:
*Amadeus – Peter Shaffer
Crimes of the Heart – Beth Henley
Fifth of July – Lanford Wilson
Mass Appeal – Bill C. Davis

Evening Standard Theatre Award for Best Play:
The Dresser – Ronald Harwood

Evening Standard Theatre Award for Best Comedy:
Make and Break – Michael Frayn

Laurence Olivier Award nominations for Best Play of the Year:
A Lesson from Aloes – Athol Fugard
Duet for One – Tom Kempinski
The Dresser – Ronald Harwood
*The Life and Adventures of Nicholas Nickleby – David Edgar, from the novel
    by Charles Dickens

Laurence Olivier Award nominations for Best Comedy of the Year:
Born in the Gardens – Peter Nichols
*Educating Rita – Willy Russell
Make and Break – Michael Frayn
Sisterly Feelings – Alan Ayckbourn

1981

The Pulitzer Prize for Drama:
A Soldier's Play – Charles Fuller

Tony Award nominations for Best Play:
Crimes of the Heart – Beth Henley
Master Harold and the Boys – Athol Fugard
The Dresser – Ronald Harwood
*The Life and Adventures of Nicholas Nickleby – David Edgar, from the novel
    by Charles Dickens

Drama Desk Award nominations for Outstanding New Play:
A Soldier's Play – Charles Fuller
The Dance and the Railroad – David Henry Hwang
Family Devotions – David Henry Hwang
Grown Ups – Jules Feiffer
*Master Harold and the Boys – Athol Fugard
The Dining Room – A.R. Gurney
Torch Song Trilogy – Harvey Fierstein

Evening Standard Theatre Award for Best Play:
Passion Play – Peter Nichols

Evening Standard Theatre Award for Best Comedy:
Goose Pimples – Mike Leigh

Laurence Olivier Award nominations for Best Play of the Year:
*Children of a Lesser God – Mark Medoff
Passion Play – Peter Nichols
Quartermaine's Terms – Simon Gray
Translations – Brian Friel

Laurence Olivier Award nominations for Best Comedy of the Year:
Anyone for Denis? – John Wells
Can't Pay? Won't Pay! – Dario Fo, translated by Lino Pertile, Bill Conville, Robert Walker
On the Razzle – Tom Stoppard
*Steaming – Nell Dunn

1982

The Pulitzer Prize for Drama:
'Night Mother: A Play – Marsha Norman

Tony Award nominations for Best Play:
Angels Fall – Lanford Wilson
'Night Mother: A Play – Marsha Norman
Plenty – David Hare
*Torch Song Trilogy – Harvey Fierstein

Drama Desk Award nominations for Outstanding New Play:
Brighton Beach Memoirs – Neil Simon
Edmund – David Mamet
Extremities – William Mastrosimone
Geniuses – Jonathan Reynolds
*Torch Song Trilogy – Harvey Fierstein
True West – Sam Shepard

Evening Standard Theatre Award for Best Play:
The Real Thing – Tom Stoppard

Evening Standard Theatre Award for Best Comedy:
Noises Off – Michael Frayn

Laurence Olivier Award nominations for Best Play of the Year:
84 Charing Cross Road – James Roose Evans, from the book by Helene Hanff
*Another Country – Julian Mitchell
Our Friends in the North – Peter Flannery

Laurence Olivier Award nominations for Best Comedy of the Year:
Key for Two – Dave Freeman, John Chapman
*Noises Off – Michael Frayn
Season's Greetings – Alan Ayckbourn
Trafford Tanzi – Claire Luckham

1983

The Pulitzer Prize for Drama:
Glengarry Glen Ross – David Mamet

Tony Award nominations for Best Play:
Glengarry Glen Ross – David Mamet
Noises Off – Michael Frayn
Play Memory – Joanna Glass
*The Real Thing – Tom Stoppard

Drama Desk Award nominations for Outstanding New Play:
A Private View – Vaclav Havel
And a Nightingale Sang – C.P. Taylor
Glengarry Glen Ross – David Mamet
Isn't It Romantic – Wendy Wasserstein
Noises Off – Michael Frayn
*The Real Thing – Tom Stoppard

Evening Standard Theatre Award for Best Play:
Master Harold and the Boys – Athol Fugard

Evening Standard Theatre Award for Best Comedy:
Tales from Hollywood – Christopher Hampton

Laurence Olivier Award nominations for Best Play of the Year:
A Pack of Lies – Hugh Whitemore
*Glengarry Glen Ross – David Mamet
Tales from Hollywood – Christopher Hampton
The Slab Boys – John Byrne

Laurence Olivier Award nominations for Best Comedy of the Year:
Beethoven's Tenth – Peter Ustinov
*Daisy Pulls It Off – Denise Deegan
Run for Your Wife – Ray Cooney
Woza Albert! – Barney Simon, Percy Mtwa, Mbongeni Ngema

1984

The Pulitzer Prize for Drama:
Sunday in the Park with George – Stephen Sondheim and James Lapine

Tony Award nominations for Best Play:
As Is – William M. Hoffman
*Biloxi Blues – Neil Simon
Hurlyburly – David Rabe
Ma Rainey's Black Bottom – August Wilson

Drama Desk Award nominations for Outstanding New Play:
*As Is – William F. Hoffman
Biloxi Blues – Neil Simon
Digby – Joseph Dougherty
Ma Rainey's Black Bottom – August Wilson

Evening Standard Theatre Award for Best Play:
Benefactors – Michael Frayn

Evening Standard Theatre Award for Best Comedy:
Stepping Out – Richard Harris

Laurence Olivier Award nominations for Best Play of the Year:

*Benefactors – Michael Frayn

Master Harold and the Boys – Athol Fugard

Poppie Nongena – Elsa Joubert, Sandra Kotze

Rat in the Skull – Ron Hutchinson

Laurence Olivier Award nominations for Best Comedy of the Year:

Gymslip Vicar – Cliffhanger Theatre Company

Intimate Exchanges – Alan Ayckbourn

Two Into One – Ray Cooney

*Up 'N' Under – John Godber

1985

The Pulitzer Prize for Drama:
Not awarded

Tony Award nominations for Best Play:

Benefactors – Michael Frayn

Blood Knot – Athol Fugard

*I'm Not Rappaport – Herb Gardner

The House of Blue Leaves – John Guare

Drama Desk Award nominations for Outstanding New Play:

*A Lie of the Mind – Sam Shepard

Aunt Dan and Lemon – Wallace Shawn

Benefactors – Michael Frayn

Execution of Justice – Emily Mann

Precious Sons – George Furth

The Marriage of Bette and Boo – Christopher Durang

Evening Standard Theatre Award for Best Play:
Pravda – Howard Brenton, David Hare

Evening Standard Theatre Award for Best Comedy:
A Chorus of Disapproval – Alan Ayckbourn

Laurence Olivier Award nominations for Best Play of the Year:

Doomsday – Tony Harrison

*Red Noses – Peter Barnes

The Road to Mecca – Athol Fugard

Torch Song Trilogy – Harvey Fierstein

Laurence Olivier Award nominations for Best Comedy of the Year:

*A Chorus of Disapproval – Alan Ayckbourn

Bouncers – John Godber

Love's Labours Lost – William Shakespeare

Pravda – Howard Brenton, David Hare

1986

The Pulitzer Prize for Drama:

Fences – August Wilson

Tony Award nominations for Best Play:

Broadway Bound – Neil Simon

Coastal Disturbances – Tina Howe

*Fences – August Wilson

Les Liaisons Dangereuses – Christopher Hampton, from the novel by Choderlos de Laclos

Drama Desk Award nominations for Outstanding New Play:

Broadway Bound – Neil Simon

Driving Miss Daisy – Alfred Uhry

*Fences – August Wilson

Les Liaisons Dangereuses – Christopher Hampton, from the novel by Choderlos de Laclos

North Shore Fish – Israel Horovitz

The Common Pursuit – Simon Gray

Wild Honey – Michael Frayn

Evening Standard Theatre Award for Best Play:

Les Liaisons Dangereuses – Christopher Hampton, from the novel by Choderlos de Laclos

A Month of Sundays – Bob Larbey

Laurence Olivier Award nominations for Best Play of the Year:
*Les Liaisons Dangereuses – Christopher Hampton, from the novel by
     Choderlos de Laclos
Ourselves Alone – Anne Devlin
The American Clock – Arthur Miller
The Normal Heart – Larry Kramer

Laurence Olivier Award nominations for Best Comedy of the Year:
A Midsummer Night's Dream – William Shakespeare
Lend Me a Tenor – Ken Ludwig
The Merry Wives of Windsor – William Shakespeare
*When We Are Married – J.B. Priestley

1987

The Pulitzer Prize for Drama:
Driving Miss Daisy – Alfred Uhry

Tony Award nominations for Best Play:
A Walk in the Woods – Lee Blessing
Joe Turner's Come and Gone – August Wilson
*M. Butterfly – David Henry Hwang
Speed the Plow – David Mamet

Drama Desk Award nominations for Outstanding New Play:
Boys' Life – Howard Korder
Joe Turner's Come and Gone – August Wilson
*M. Butterfly – David Henry Hwang
Speed the Plow – David Mamet
The Road to Mecca – Athol Fugard
Women in Mind – Alan Ayckbourn

Evening Standard Theatre Award for Best Play:
A Small Family Business – Alan Ayckbourn

Evening Standard Theatre Award for Best Comedy:
Serious Money – Caryl Churchill

Laurence Olivier Award nominations for Best Play of the Year:
A Lie of the Mind – Sam Shepard
Lettice and Lovage – Peter Shaffer
Sarcophagus – Vladimir Gubaryev
*Serious Money – Caryl Churchill

Laurence Olivier Award nominations for Best Comedy of the Year:
A Midsummer Night's Dream – William Shakespeare
Groucho – Arthur Marx, Robert Fisher
*Three Men on a Horse – John Cecil Holm, George Abbott
Twelfth Night – William Shakespeare

1988

The Pulitzer Prize for Drama:
The Heidi Chronicles – Wendy Wasserstein

Tony Award nominations for Best Play:
Largely New York – Bill Irwin
Lend Me a Tenor – Ken Ludwig
Shirley Valentine – Willy Russell
*The Heidi Chronicles – Wendy Wasserstein

Drama Desk Award nominations for Outstanding New Play:
Only Kidding – Jim Geoghan
Reckless – Craig Lucas
Shirley Valentine – Willy Russell
The Cocktail Hour – A.R. Gurney
The Film Society – Jon Robin Baitz
*The Heidi Chronicles – Wendy Wasserstein

Evening Standard Theatre Award for Best Play:
Aristocrats – Brian Friel

Evening Standard Theatre Award for Best Comedy:
Lettice and Lovage – Peter Shaffer

Laurence Olivier Award nominations for Best Play of the Year:

A Walk in the Woods – Lee Blessing

Mrs. Klein – Nicholas Wright

*Our Country's Good – Timberlake Wertenbaker

The Secret Rapture – David Hare

Laurence Olivier Award nominations for Best Comedy of the Year:

Henceforward – Alan Ayckbourn

Separation – Tom Kempinski

*Shirley Valentine – Willy Russell

The Common Pursuit – Simon Gray

1989

The Pulitzer Prize for Drama:

The Piano Lesson – August Wilson

Tony Award nominations for Best Play:

Lettice and Lovage – Peter Shaffer

Prelude to a Kiss – Craig Lucas

*The Grapes of Wrath – Frank Galati, from the novel by John Steinbeck

The Piano Lesson – August Wilson

Drama Desk Award nominations for Outstanding New Play:

Prelude to a Kiss – Craig Lucas

Some Americans Abroad – Richard Nelson

The Lisbon Traviata – Terrence McNally

*The Piano Lesson – August Wilson

The Secret Rapture – David Hare

Evening Standard Theatre Award for Best Play:

Ghetto – Joshua Sobol

Evening Standard Theatre Award for Best Comedy:

Henceforward – Alan Ayckbourn

Laurence Olivier Award nominations for Best New Play:
Ghetto – Joshua Sobol
Man of the Moment – Alan Ayckbourn
*Racing Demon – David Hare
Shadowlands – William Nicholson

Laurence Olivier Award nominations for Comedy of the Year:
*Single Spies – Alan Bennett
Some Americans Abroad – Richard Nelson
Steel Magnolias – Robert Harling
Jeffrey Bernard is Unwell – Keith Waterhouse

1990

The Pulitzer Prize for Drama:
Lost in Yonkers – Neil Simon

Tony Award nominations for Best Play:
*Lost in Yonkers – Neil Simon
Our Country's Good – Timberlake Wertenbaker
Shadowlands – William Nicholson
Six Degrees of Separation – John Guare

Drama Desk Award nominations for Outstanding New Play:
La Bête – David Hirson
*Lost in Yonkers – Neil Simon
Six Degrees of Separation – John Guare
The Wash – Philip Kan Gotanda

Evening Standard Theatre Award for Best Play:
Shadowlands – William Nicholson

Evening Standard Theatre Award for Best Comedy:
Man of the Moment – Alan Ayckbourn
Jeffrey Bernard is Unwell – Keith Waterhouse

Laurence Olivier Award nominations for Best New Play:
*Dancing at Lughnasa – Brian Friel
Singer – Peter Flannery
The Trackers of Oxyrhynchus – Tony Harrison
White Chameleon – Christopher Hampton

Laurence Olivier Award nominations for Best Comedy:
Gasping – Ben Elton
*Out of Order – Ray Cooney

1991

The Pulitzer Prize for Drama:
The Kentucky Cycle – Robert Schenkkan

Tony Award nominations for Best Play:
*Dancing at Lughnasa – Brian Friel
Four Baboons Adoring the Sun – John Guare
Two Shakespearean Actors – Richard Nelson
Two Trains Running – August Wilson

Drama Desk Award nominations for Outstanding New Play:
A Small Family Business – Alan Ayckbourn
Dancing at Lughnasa – Brian Friel
Lips Together, Teeth Apart – Terrence McNally
Mad Forest – Caryl Churchill
*Marvin's Room – Scott McPherson
Sight Unseen – Donald Margulies

Evening Standard Theatre Award for Best Play:
Dancing at Lughnasa – Brian Friel

Evening Standard Theatre Award for Best Comedy:
Kvetch – Steven Berkoff

Laurence Olivier Award nominations for Best New Play:
Angels in America: Millennium Approaches – Tony Kushner
*Death and the Maiden – Ariel Dorfman
The Madness of George III – Alan Bennett
Three Birds Alighting on a Field – Timberlake Wertenbaker

Laurence Olivier Award nominations for Best Comedy:
An Evening with Gary Lineker – Arthur Smith, Chris England
It's Ralph – Hugh Whitemore
*La Bête – David Hirson

1992

The Pulitzer Prize for Drama:
Angels in America: Millennium Approaches – Tony Kushner

Tony Award nominations for Best Play:
*Angels in America: Millennium Approaches – Tony Kushner
Someone Who'll Watch Over Me – Frank McGuinness
The Sisters Rosensweig – Wendy Wasserstein
The Song of Jacob Zulu – Tug Yourgrau

Drama Desk Award nominations for Outstanding New Play:
*Angels in America: Millennium Approaches – Tony Kushner
Jeffrey – Paul Rudnick
Joined at the Head – Catherine Butterfield
Oleanna – David Mamet
The Sisters Rosensweig – Wendy Wasserstein
Three Hotels – Jon Robin Baitz

Evening Standard Theatre Award for Best Play:
Angels in America: Millennium Approaches – Tony Kushner

Evening Standard Theatre Award for Best Comedy:
The Rise and Fall of Little Voice – Jim Cartwright

Laurence Olivier Award nominations for Best New Play:

*Six Degrees of Separation** – John Guare

Someone Who'll Watch Over Me** – Frank McGuinness

The Gift of the Gorgon** – Peter Shaffer

The Street of Crocodiles** – Théâtre de Complicité, from stories by Bruno Sculz

Laurence Olivier Award nominations for Best Comedy:

Lost in Yonkers** – Neil Simon

On the Piste** – John Godber

*The Rise and Fall of Little Voice** – Jim Cartwright

1993

The Pulitzer Prize for Drama:

Three Tall Women** – Edward Albee

Tony Award nominations for Best Play:

*Angels in America: Perestroika** – Tony Kushner

Broken Glass** – Arthur Miller

The Kentucky Cycle** – Robert Schenkkan

Twilight: Los Angeles, 1992** – Anna Deavere Smith

Drama Desk Award nominations for Outstanding Play:

*Angels in America: Perestroika** – Tony Kushner

All in the Timing** – David Ives

The Kentucky Cycle** – Robert Schenkkan

The Lights** – Howard Korder

Pterodactyls** – Nicky Silver

Evening Standard Theatre Award for Best Play:

Arcadia** – Tom Stoppard

Evening Standard Theatre Award for Best Comedy:

Jamais Vu** – Ken Campbell

Laurence Olivier Award nominations for Best New Play:

Angels in America: Perestroika – Tony Kushner

*Arcadia – Tom Stoppard

Oleanna – David Mamet

The Last Yankee – Arthur Miller

Laurence Olivier Award nominations for Best Comedy:

April in Paris – John Godber

*Hysteria – Terry Johnson

The Life of Stuff – Simon Donald

Time of My Life – Alan Ayckbourn

1994

The Pulitzer Prize for Drama:

The Young Man from Atlanta – Horton Foote

Tony Award nominations for Best Play:

Arcadia – Tom Stoppard

Having Our Say – Emily Mann

Indiscretions – Jean Cocteau, translated by Jeremy Sams

*Love! Valour! Compassion! – Terrence McNally

Drama Desk Award nominations for Outstanding Play:

Arcadia – Tom Stoppard

*Love! Valour! Compassion! – Terrence McNally

Missing Persons – Craig Lucas

Raised in Captivity – Nicky Silver

SubUrbia – Eric Bogosian

The Cryptogram – David Mamet

Evening Standard Theatre Award for Best Play:

Three Tall Women – Edward Albee

Evening Standard Theatre Award for Best Comedy:

My Night with Reg – Kevin Elyot

Laurence Olivier Award nominations for Best New Play:

900 Oneonta – David Beaird

*Broken Glass – Arthur Miller

Dealer's Choice – Patrick Marber

Three Tall Women – Edward Albee

Laurence Olivier Award nominations for Best Comedy:

Beautiful Thing – Jonathan Harvey

Dead Funny – Terry Johnson

*My Night with Reg – Kevin Elyot

Neville's Island – Tim Firth

1995

The Pulitzer Prize for Drama:

Rent – Jonathan Larson

Tony Award nominations for Best Play:

Buried Child – Sam Shepard

*Master Class – Terrence McNally

Racing Demon – David Hare

Seven Guitars – August Wilson

Drama Desk Award nominations for Outstanding Play:

*Master Class – Terrence McNally

Molly Sweeney – Brian Friel

Seven Guitars – August Wilson

Sylvia – A.R. Gurney

The Model Apartment – Donald Margulies

Valley Song – Athol Fugard

Evening Standard Theatre Award for Best Play:

Pentecost – David Edgar

Evening Standard Theatre Award for Best Comedy:

Dealer's Choice – Patrick Marber

Laurence Olivier Award nominations for Best New Play:

Pentecost – David Edgar

*Skylight – David Hare

Taking Sides – Ronald Harwood

The Steward of Christendom – Sebastian Barry

Laurence Olivier Award nominations for Best Comedy:

Communicating Doors – Alan Ayckbourn

Funny Money – Ray Cooney

*Mojo – Jez Butterworth

1996

The Pulitzer Prize for Drama:
No award

Tony Award nominations for Best Play:
Skylight – David Hare
Stanley – Pam Gems
*The Last Night of Ballyhoo – Alfred Uhry
The Young Man from Atlanta – Horton Foote

Drama Desk Award nominations for Outstanding New Play:
Dealer's Choice – Patrick Marber
*How I Learned to Drive – Paula Vogel
The Last Night of Ballyhoo – Alfred Uhry
The Skriker – Caryl Churchill
This Is Our Youth – Kenneth Lonergan

Evening Standard Theatre Award for Best Play:
Stanley – Pam Gems

Evening Standard Theatre Award for Best Comedy:
Art – Yasmina Reza, translated by Christopher Hampton

Laurence Olivier Award nominations for Best New Play:

Blinded by the Sun – Stephen Poliakoff

*Stanley – Pam Gems

The Beauty Queen of Leenane – Martin McDonagh

The Herbal Bed – Peter Whelan

Laurence Olivier Award nominations for Best Comedy:

*Art – Yasmina Reza, translated by Christopher Hampton

Laughter on the 23rd Floor – Neil Simon

The Complete Works of William Shakespeare (abridged) – A. Long, D. Singer, J. Winfield

1997

The Pulitzer Prize for Drama:

How I Learned to Drive – Paula Vogel

Tony Award nominations for Best Play:

*Art – Yasmina Reza, translated by Christopher Hampton

Freak – John Leguizamo

Golden Child – David Henry Hwang

The Beauty Queen of Leenane – Martin McDonagh

Drama Desk Award nominations for Outstanding Play:

Art – Yasmina Reza, translated by Christopher Hampton

As Bees in Honey Drown – Douglas Carter Beane

Collected Stories – Donald Margulies

Side Man – Warren Leight

*The Beauty Queen of Leenane – Martin McDonagh

Three Days of Rain – Richard Greenberg

Evening Standard Theatre Award for Best Play:

The Invention of Love – Tom Stoppard

Evening Standard Theatre Award for Best Comedy:

Closer – Patrick Marber

Laurence Olivier Award nominations for Best New Play:

Amy's View – David Hare

*Closer – Patrick Marber

Hurlyburly – David Rabe

The Invention of Love – Tom Stoppard

Tom and Clem – Stephen Churchett

Laurence Olivier Award nominations for Best New Comedy:

A Skull in Connemara – Martin McDonagh

East is East – Ayub Khan-Din

*Popcorn – Ben Elton

1998

The Pulitzer Prize for Drama:

Wit – Margaret Edson

Tony Award nominations for Best Play:

Closer – Patrick Marber

Not About Nightingales – Tennessee Williams

*Side Man – Warren Leight

The Lonesome West – Martin McDonagh

Drama Desk Award nominations for Outstanding Play:

Betty's Summer Vacation – Christopher Durang

Closer – Patrick Marber

Not About Nightingales – Tennessee Williams

Snakebit – David Marshall Grant

The Ride Down Mount Morgan – Arthur Miller

*Wit – Margaret Edson

Evening Standard Theatre Award for Best Play:

Copenhagen – Michael Frayn

Evening Standard Theatre Award for Best Comedy:

No award

Copenhagen – Michael Frayn
The Blue Room – David Hare
The Unexpected Man – Yasmina Reza, translated by Christopher Hampton
*The Weir – Conor McPherson

Laurence Olivier Award nominations for Best New Comedy:

Alarms and Excursions – Michael Frayn
*Cleo, Camping, Emmanuelle and Dick – Terry Johnson
Love upon the Throne – Patrick Barlow
Things We Do For Love – Alan Ayckbourn

1999

The Pulitzer Prize for Drama:
Dinner with Friends – Donald Margulies

Tony Award nominations for Best Play:
*Copenhagen – Michael Frayn
Dirty Blonde – Claudia Shear
The Ride Down Mount Morgan – Arthur Miller
True West – Sam Shepard

Drama Desk Award nominations for Outstanding New Play:
Contact – Frank Gilroy
*Copenhagen – Michael Frayn
Dinner with Friends – Donald Margulies
Dirty Blonde – Claudia Shear
Jitney – August Wilson
The Tale of the Allergist's Wife – Charles Busch

Evening Standard Theatre Award for Best Play:
No award

Evening Standard Theatre Award for Best Comedy:
No award

Laurence Olivier Award nominations for Best New Play:

*Goodnight Children Everywhere – Richard Nelson

Perfect Days – Liz Lochhead

Rose – Martin Sherman

The Lady in the Van – Alan Bennett

Three Days of Rain – Richard Greenberg

Laurence Olivier Award nominations for Best New Comedy:

Comic Potential – Alan Ayckbourn

Quartet – Ronald Harwood

*The Memory of Water – Shelagh Stephenson

2000

The Pulitzer Prize for Drama:

Proof – David Auburn

Tony Award nominations for Best Play:

King Hedley II – August Wilson

*Proof – David Auburn

The Invention of Love – Tom Stoppard

The Tale of the Allergist's Wife – Charles Busch

Drama Desk Award nominations for Outstanding Play:

Boy Gets Girl – Rebecca Gilman

Comic Potential – Alan Ayckbourn

Lobby Hero – Kenneth Lonergan

*Proof – David Auburn

The Invention of Love – Tom Stoppard

The Unexpected Man – Yasmina Reza, translated by Christopher Hampton

Evening Standard Theatre Award for Best Play:

Blue/Orange – Joe Penhall

Evening Standard Theatre Award for Best Comedy:

Stones in His Pockets – Marie Jones

Laurence Olivier Award nominations for Best New Play:

*Blue/Orange – Joe Penhall
Dolly West's Kitchen – Frank McGuinness
Life x 3 – Yasmina Reza, translated by Christopher Hampton
My Zinc Bed – David Hare

Laurence Olivier Award nominations for Best New Comedy:

Cooking with Elvis – Lee Hall
House/Garden – Alan Ayckbourn
Peggy for You – Alan Plater
*Stones in His Pockets – Marie Jones

2001

The Pulitzer Prize for Drama:

Topdog/Underdog – Suzan-Lori Parks

Tony Award nominations for Best Play:

Fortune's Fool – by Ivan Turgenev, adapted by Mike Poulton
Metamorphoses – Mary Zimmerman
*The Goat or Who Is Sylvia? – Edward Albee
Topdog/Underdog – Suzan-Lori Parks

Drama Desk Award nominations for Outstanding Play:

Franny's Way – Richard Nelson
*Metamorphoses – Mary Zimmerman
*The Goat or Who Is Sylvia? – Edward Albee
The Shape of Things – Neil LaBute
Thief River – Lee Blessing
Topdog/Underdog – Suzan-Lori Parks

Evening Standard Theatre Award nominations for Best Play:

*The Far Side of the Moon – Robert Lepage
Mouth to Mouth – Kevin Elyot
The Shape of Things – Neil LaBute

Evening Standard Theatre Award nominations for Best Comedy:

Caught in the Net – Ray Cooney
*Feelgood – Alistair Beaton
Life x 3 – Yasmina Reza , translated by Christopher Hampton

Laurence Olivier Award nominations for Best New Play:

Boy Gets Girl – Rebecca Gilman
Gagarin Way – Gregory Burke
Humble Boy – Charlotte Jones
*Jitney – August Wilson
Mouth to Mouth – Kevin Elyot

Laurence Olivier Award nominations for Best New Comedy:

Boston Marriage – David Mamet
Caught in the Net – Ray Cooney
Feelgood – Alistair Beaton
*The Play What I Wrote – Hamish McColl, Sean Foley, Eddie Braben

2002

The Pulitzer Prize for Drama:
Anna in the Tropics – Nilo Cruz

Tony Award nominations for Best Play:

Enchanted April – Matthew Barber
Say Goodnight, Gracie – Rupert Holmes
*Take Me Out – Richard Greenberg
Vincent in Brixton – Nicholas Wright

Drama Desk Award nominations for Outstanding Play:

Buicks – Julian Sheppard
Our Lady of 121st Street – Stephen Adly Guirgis
Peter and Vandy – Jay DiPietro
*Take Me Out – Richard Greenberg
Talking Heads – Alan Bennett
Yellowman – Dael Orlandersmith

Evening Standard Theatre Award nominations for Best Play:

*A Number – Caryl Churchill

The Lieutenant of Inishmore – Martin McDonagh

The York Realist – Peter Gill

Laurence Olivier Award nominations for Best New Play:

Jesus Hopped the 'A' Train – Stephen Adly Guirgis

The Coast of Utopia – Voyage, Shipwreck, Salvage – Tom Stoppard

The York Realist – Peter Gill

*Vincent in Brixton – Nicholas Wright

Laurence Olivier Award nominations for Best New Comedy:

Damsels in Distress – Roleplay – Alan Ayckbourn

Dinner – Moira Buffini

Lobby Hero – Kenneth Lonergan

*The Lieutenant of Inishmore – Martin McDonagh

2003

The Pulitzer Prize for Drama:

I Am My Own Wife – Doug Wright

Tony Award nominations for Best Play:

Anna in the Tropics – Nilo Cruz

Frozen – Bryony Lavery

*I Am My Own Wife – Doug Wright

The Retreat from Moscow – William Nicholson

Drama Desk Award nominations for Outstanding Play:

Humble Boy – Charlotte Jones

*I Am My Own Wife – Doug Wright

Moby Dick – Julian Rad

The Beard of Avon – Amy Freed

The Distance from Here – Neil LaBute

The Tricky Part – Martin Moran

Evening Standard Theatre Award nominations for Best Play:

*Democracy – Michael Frayn

After Mrs Rochester – Polly Teale

Fallout – Roy Williams

Laurence Olivier Award nominations for Best New Play:

Democracy – Michael Frayn

Elmina's Kitchen – Kwame Kwei-Armah

Hitchcock Blonde – Terry Johnson

*The Pillowman – Martin McDonagh

2004

The Pulitzer Prize for Drama:

Doubt, A Parable – John Patrick Shanley

Tony Award nominations for Best Play:

Democracy – Michael Frayn

*Doubt, A Parable – John Patrick Shanley

Gem of the Ocean – August Wilson

The Pillowman – Martin McDonagh

Drama Desk Award nominations for Outstanding Play:

Democracy – Michael Frayn

*Doubt, A Parable – John Patrick Shanley

Pentecost – David Edgar

The Pillowman – Martin McDonagh

Sailor's Song – John Patrick Shanley

Sin (A Cardinal Deposed) – Michael Murphy

Evening Standard Theatre Award nominations for Best Play:

The Goat or Who is Sylvia? – Edward Albee

*The History Boys – Alan Bennett

The Pillowman – Martin McDonagh

Laurence Olivier Award nominations for Best New Play:

By the Bog of Cats – Marina Carr

Festen – David Eldridge, from the film and play by Thomas Vinterberg, Morgens Rukov, Bo hr. Hansen

The Goat or Who Is Sylvia? – Edward Albee

*The History Boys – Alan Bennett

2005

The Pulitzer Prize for Drama:
No award

Tony Award nominations for Best Play:
*The History Boys – Alan Bennett
The Lieutenant of Inishmore – Martin McDonagh
Rabbit Hole – David Lindsay-Abaire
Shining City – Conor McPherson

Drama Desk Award nominations for Outstanding Play:
*The History Boys – Alan Bennett
Stuff Happens – David Hare
No Foreigners Beyond this Point – Warren Leight
The Lieutenant of Inishmore – Martin McDonagh
Dedication or the Stuff of Dreams – Terrence McNally
The Pavilion – Craig Wright

Evening Standard Theatre Award nominations for Best Play:
2000 Years – Mike Leigh
Bloody Sunday – Richard Norton-Taylor
Harvest – Richard Bean
*The Home Place – Brian Friel

Laurence Olivier Award nominations for Best New Play:
Coram Boy – Helen Edmundson, from the novel by Jamila Gavin
Harvest – Richard Bean
*On the Shore of the Wide World – Simon Stephens
Paul – Howard Brenton

Laurence Olivier Award nominations for Best New Comedy:
Glorious! – Peter Quilter
*Heroes – Gérald Sibleyras, translated by Tom Stoppard
Shoot the Crow – Owen McCafferty

2006

The Pulitzer Prize for Drama:
Rabbit Hole – David Lindsay-Abaire

Tony Award nominations for Best Play:
The Little Dog Laughed – Douglas Carter Beane
Frost/Nixon – Peter Morgan
*The Coast of Utopia – Tom Stoppard
Radio Golf – August Wilson

Drama Desk Award nominations for Outstanding Play:
Blackbird – David Harrower
Some Men – Terrence McNally
Frost/Nixon – Peter Morgan
*The Coast of Utopia – Tom Stoppard
The Accomplices – Bernard Weinraub
Radio Golf – August Wilson

Evening Standard Theatre Award nominations for Best Play:
Frost/Nixon – Peter Morgan
*Rock 'N' Roll – Tom Stoppard
The Seafarer – Conor McPherson

Laurence Olivier Award nominations for Best New Play:
*Blackbird – David Harrower
Frost/Nixon – Peter Morgan
Rock 'N' Roll – Tom Stoppard
The Seafarer – Conor McPherson

Laurence Olivier Award nominations for Best New Comedy:
*The 39 Steps – Patrick Barlow, from the novel by John Buchan
Don Juan in Soho – Patrick Marber, from the play by Molière
Love Song – John Kolvenbach